RAW
crafts

CALGARY PUBLIC LIBRARY

MAR   2017

D0471860

New York

An Imprint of Sterling Publishing
1166 Avenue of the Americas
New York, NY 10036

LARK CRAFTS and the distinctive Lark
logo are registered trademarks of Sterling
Publishing Co., Inc.

© 2015 by RotoVision SA

Photography by Neal Grundy
Illustrations by Sarah Lawrence

All rights reserved. No part of this publication
may be reproduced, stored in a retrieval
system, or transmitted in any form or by any
means (including electronic, mechanical,
photocopying, recording, or otherwise) without
prior written permission from the publisher.

ISBN 978-1-4547-0929-9

Distributed in Canada by Sterling Publishing
c/o Canadian Manda Group, 664 Annette Street
Toronto, Ontario, Canada M6S 2C8

For information about custom editions, special
sales, and premium and corporate purchases,
please contact Sterling Special Sales at 800-805-
5489 or specialsales@sterlingpublishing.com.

Every effort has been made to ensure that
all the information in this book is accurate.
However, due to differing conditions, tools,
and individual skills, the publisher cannot be
responsible for any injuries, losses, and other
damages that may result from the use of the
information in this book.

Manufactured in China

2 4 6 8 10 9 7 5 3 1

larkcrafts.com

RAW
crafts

40 PROJECTS from HEMP, JUTE, BURLAP, and CORK

DENISE CORCORAN

LARK
New York

Contents

Chapter 5

DECORATIONS & EMBELLISHMENTS 112

Chapter 6

RESOURCES 136

Introduction

Crafting and upcycling are the new "it" hobbies. Meeting up with friends and knitting or creating your very own macramé signature piece is all the rage. And so are "raw" crafts. The use of natural fibers in your DIYs, especially restyling discarded items such as burlap sacks, is an exciting way to explore your creative side.

You'll find your craft supplies at your local craft store and even in dollar stores. There are simple ways to enter the maker world and you can do it on a budget and without investing a lot of time. The beauty of this new frontier is that you come across something you want to create, find or buy the materials you need, and then take the plunge. Handmade is not meant to be perfect; it is meant to be a happy treasure that you craft in your own way and in your own time, and then joyfully reveal.

The projects in this book are perfect for incorporating upcycled or restyled finds. Set aside a day so that you can rummage the shelves in some local thrift stores, sift through your recycle bin, collect miscellaneous buttons and beads, and generally forage cupboards for useful items. Surrounded by a treasure trove of things and fueled up on inspiration, you are ready to upcycle and craft. Enjoy the adventure of creating something amazing from a piece of jute and a few beads, for example. Who would have believed that macramé could be so awesome!

Try each of the signature materials—burlap, cork, jute, and hemp—and see what works best. Then mix and match the materials, trying different combinations. Burlap could be your new best friend when it comes to running up a curtain, and cork the dream material for making stunning jewelry. Jute might be your go-to material for a hanging macramé vase, while hemp is the braided core of the beaded bracelets that you gift to your friends. Try one signature material, and then try them all!

My hope is that you'll enjoy making the projects as much as I did, and that you'll share your projects, your ideas, and your passion for crafting. But there should be a loud cheer for the whole reality of upcycling and making stuff out of "junk." Happy making, my new crafty friends! I have no doubt you'll find many projects in this book that will inspire you to keep creating. Enjoy!

Denise Corcoran

How to use this book

The one thing I hope to instil in you is that crafting and upcycling is fun. No project is meant to be perfect or created in the same way by everyone. Take the instructions in this book as a guide only. When making a project for the first time, follow the steps to start, but as in any recipe there is always a way to improve and enhance so that the finished make shows your personality. Skip steps, add steps, and substitute materials; and if you have a craft disaster, please try again. We are all creative creatures and with a little bit of money and time there is no limit to what we can make. And don't talk yourself down. Handmade things wear their imperfections with pride. Revel in your successes, learn (or laugh in my case) from the disasters, but mainly enjoy!

I've tried in most projects to suggest how to repurpose old or second-hand items. This is not how everyone will want to craft, but I find that by reusing you save money, waste less, and can make something that is totally unique. Feel free to follow this mantra or ignore it; there are no hard and fast rules in crafting.

In this book you'll find options for adding the "wow" factor to your DIYs, but you should definitely experiment with other options and look at ways of customizing your projects. I've also added suggestions on combining elements of different projects together. You'll find these under the heading "Craft Mix and Match." Simply check out the choices and see which appeals to you. You may even unearth your own mix and match combinations. Be open to the adventure—there is nothing to lose when you craft. If there is a technique or a process that is not mentioned in this book, there's always the library, the bookshop, a craft collective, and the Internet. At the end of the book there is a resource section that recommends good sources of information and inspiration.

Tools and materials

The projects in this book don't require a tool shed, workshop, or studio of equipment, and what you do need you most probably already have...somewhere! Just as you give some materials a second life in your projects, those tools that languished in a drawer may also get their chance to shine.

Clipboard When doing knotting and beading using jute and hemp, it's really helpful to be able to secure one end of the macramé under the clamp of a clipboard. The alternative is to hammer a nail or fix a screw hook into a piece of board (letter paper or A4 size is pretty good), and to secure the cords to the nail or hook.

Craft knife This is the go-to knife for cutting wine corks and cork sheets, and just about everything else as far as raw crafts are concerned. Be careful when using them and keep spare blades to hand. A dull blade means a messy cut and no fun.

Cutting mat Trust me—a mat cutting board is worth the investment. It's perfect for cutting cork, cardboard, and balsa. The mat won't wear or show cuts, plus it has grid lines that'll help you cut straight lines and right angles.

Darning needle This needle with a large eye is perfect when working with thick cords like hemp or jute. If you want to hand-stitch burlap, I recommend hemp or jute threaded into a darning needle. Craft stores sell sets of darning needles.

Dressmaking pins You can never pin enough if it helps you create a craft masterpiece.

Dye Read the packaging instructions before investing in a commercial dye product. Some require a lot of steps, and a large work space, so always choose the most straight-forward product. Once you've decided on a dye, get the required supplies ready and prepare a work area.

Embroidery floss and embroidery needle There are a few projects where I suggest decorating with simple embroidery stitches. You can find the needles and floss at craft stores.

Fabric glue This glue can be a good stand-in for fusible webbing, thereby foregoing any need to thread a needle or get out the sewing machine. Use fabric glue to adhere felt or other fabrics to burlap, for example. Use sparingly and allow to dry before continuing with the next step. Available at craft or fabric stores.

Fusible webbing and an iron I love fusible webbing —the best sewing invention ever! Once the webbing is sandwiched in a hem or similar, set the iron on high (don't use steam), and let the heat fuse the adhesive on the webbing to the layers of fabric. I recommend covering burlap with a piece of scrap fabric before letting the iron do its job.

Tools and materials continued

Glue gun and glue sticks Crafting and glue guns go hand in hand. They save lots of time and mess, and the glue dries faster and harder than many alternatives. It is not all that expensive, and you can pick a glue gun up pre-owned. If you are just starting out on a craft adventure, see if you can borrow one so that you try it out and discover its benefits. You can buy a glue gun and glue sticks in craft, dollar, and hardware stores. No glue gun? Then use fabric or white glue (whichever is appropriate for the materials being used), applied with a paintbrush or spongebrush.

Paintbrushes and spongebrushes You'll want to have both of these on hand for the DIYs in this book. Both can be found at craft, dollar, and hardware stores. You will need broad brushes to cover large surfaces, and narrower ones for smaller areas. Use different brushes to apply paint and glue.

Pliers One main pair of pliers or a set are perfect for crafting. You'll find that you use them all the time! When cutting wine corks (and there's quite a few to cut in this book) you may like to grip the cork in the pliers while you cut. I often do this when cutting the last few disks from the cork and my fingertips are uncomfortably near the blade. (A small vise will serve the same purpose.) Buy pliers new from a hardware store, or pre-owned at a garage sale or thrift store. If you have a tool library in your neighborhood, you can borrow them.

Scissors It's great to have a few pairs on hand. Keep one pair sharp for cutting fabric, and have a second pair to use when crafting with cord, paper, cardboard, cork, balsa, and other materials.

Sewing machine For most of the DIYs in this book you can choose to sew by hand, but it is handy to have a sewing machine available for the bigger projects.

White glue Run of the mill white glue, craft glue, or school glue—there are so many names for this product —is what you'll use in most of the DIYs. At times you may need wood glue, contact cement, cyanoacrylate glue, or even a glue stick. White glue is great for preventing the raw edges on burlap fraying, and when diluted can be painted onto a surface to add a sealing coat. A word of advice: stock up on white glue—you'll be using lots!

Work space Set yourself up in a comfy space where there is good lighting, some storage, a socket for electrical equipment, and a creative vibe. Most of the projects in this book don't require a lot of room, so set up a table with elbow room or spread yourself out on the floor.

Overview

Burlap, also known as hessian, is a rough textured, loosely woven fabric usually made from jute or hemp. Burlap's claim to fame is its use in shipping sacks for coffee beans. It's recently become the go-to material for upcycling fanatics due to its accessibility, cost (inexpensive and sometimes even free if you know a coffee roaster), and the sheer scope of its use in repurposing projects.

Over the past couple of centuries India has developed numerous uses for the fibers of the jute plant such as rope, paper, and hand-woven bags. From these burlap was developed—a strong and durable material perfect for transporting goods.

The most popular projects for this fabric are cushion covers, garden planters, wreaths, and garlands but the list grows longer almost daily as crafters find yet another application for burlap. Most craft stores stock rolls of burlap and burlap ribbons, garlands, and bags that you can customize.

The upside to burlap is its durability, while its downside is that it can be dirty, smelly, and easy to fray. As you use burlap, you will develop skills and tricks to overcome the downsides so that you can optimize this wonderfully textured material for all your craft needs. For example, to minimize fraying, brush the cut edges of the burlap with white glue or finish raw edges with a decorative edge stitch (blanket stitch) or a zigzag stitch.

Embellishing burlap is effortless and it can be customized with cross-stitch, blanket-stitch, stencils, paint, or felt appliqué. Also, feel free to have fun with your upcycled burlap by screen-printing a design. But above all, experiment, as this is the best part of crafting.

Preparing burlap sacks for use

When upcycling a burlap shipping sack, plan ahead. It is very important to remove stains, wash, and iron the raw fabric before you start on your project.

Start by shaking out the burlap to remove excess dirt and loose threads, and remove stains with laundry soap and a damp sponge. Gently rub the stain, and then wash the burlap (large pieces only) in a washing machine.

To wash large pieces of burlap, use the gentle cycle, cold water (warm water may shrink the fabric), and a little detergent. Hang or lay out to dry, but if in a hurry, pop the fabric in a tumble drier. A word of advice: once the burlap has been washed and dried, check the washing machine and drier—especially the lint tray and filter—to remove burlap threads that may clog your machines.

Do not machine wash small pieces of burlap as the turbulence may cause excessive fraying, making the piece unstable and unusable. Instead, hand wash in cold water with a gentle detergent, and then soak the burlap for five to 10 minutes. Rinse out the detergent, gently wring out excess water, and lay the burlap flat to dry. Finish preparation by ironing the burlap, using the steamer to press out any wrinkles.

Wreath

I doubt there is an easier or better use of burlap, a wire frame, and 10 minutes of your time than creating this wreath. Customize it for a special occasion, dye the burlap to match the décor, or give it a seasonal facelift with holly leaves and berries. Imagine how festive the wreath will look above a fireplace or on the front door! If you're sticking to a budget, use strips cut from an old burlap sack, otherwise buy purpose-made rolls of burlap garland from a craft store.

> CRAFT MIX AND MATCH
  Flower (page 20)
  Bird ornament (page 110)
  Dyeing (page 124)

You will need

- Burlap, 6 x 24 inches (15 x 31 cm)
- Wire wreath frame, 12 inches (30.5 cm) diameter
- Scissors
- Piece of jute or ribbon, 10 inches (25.5 cm) in length

How to make the wreath

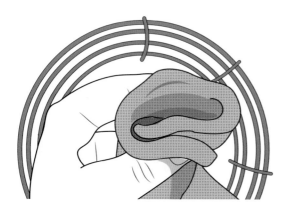

1 Fold the burlap in half lengthwise twice to form a roll measuring 1½ x 24 inches (4 x 31 cm).

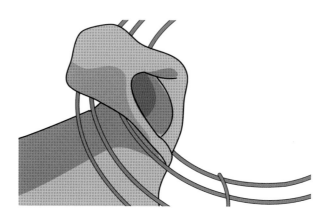

2 Lay the frame over one end of burlap roll. Pull a length of the burlap up between the innermost rings of the frame to form a small loop, leaving the end on the underside of the frame. Pull another section of the burlap up between the middle rings to make another small loop. Repeat to make a loop between the outermost rings. To give the garland an organic look, adjust the loops to make them of various heights and widths.

3 Twist the burlap (this will help the loops hold their places in the frame and make the wreath more robust) and repeat step 2 to make more loops to the right of the first loops, starting from the innermost ring and working to the outermost ring. Continue until the whole frame is covered with loops.

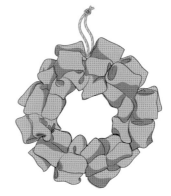

4 Make final adjustments to the loops, and trim or tuck the ends out of sight. Thread jute through the outer ring and knot the ends to make a hanging loop. Decorate with burlap flowers or the bird ornament.

Flower

There are so many ways to use this flower—as a brooch for a coat, scarf, or hat; and as decoration for a bag, frame, wreath, or napkin ring. To give the flower a stem, glue a cork disk to the bottom of the flower and insert a skewer into the cork and up into the base of the flower. Place the stems in a container or bind them together with a burlap ribbon. You can cut leaves from natural or green-dyed burlap and glue these to each stem. These flowers measure approximately 2½ inches (6.5 cm) across. To make smaller or larger flowers, simply adjust the quantities below.

> CRAFT MIX AND MATCH
  Boutonnière (page 30)
  Dyeing (page 124)

You will need

- Burlap, one piece 4 inches square (10 cm sq) and a strip 2 x 12 inches (5 x 30.5 cm) per flower
- Ruler and chalk
- Scissors
- Glue gun and glue sticks or white glue and paintbrush
- Clothespins

How to make the flower

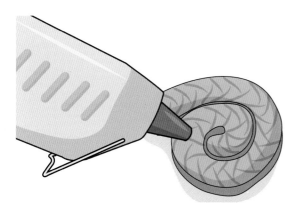

1 To make the flower center: roll up the square of burlap, so you have a long tube. Then starting at one end begin to make a tight coil. Start wrapping the coil around itself, dabbing with glue so that the coil holds its shape. Clamp with clothespins while the coil dries.

2 To make the petals: fold the burlap strip in half along its length so that the raw edges are aligned, and then fold one end over (as shown). Apply glue to hold the fold in place.

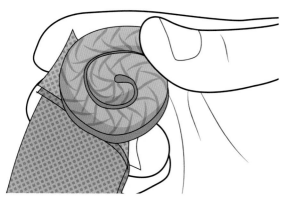

3 Glue the folded end of the burlap strip to the flower center. Wrap and glue the folded burlap strip around the flower center once, folded edge uppermost and with the strip standing proud of the center.

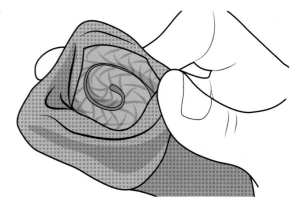

4 Continue wrapping the burlap around the center, but keep twisting the burlap to form individual petals. Apply glue to keep the petals in place. When there is about 1½ inches (4 cm) of burlap left, fold and glue it to the base of the flower. Leave to dry and then trim any stray threads.

Plant pot container

Burlap plant pot containers are urban rustic chic and all the rage! They are the perfect way to cover unsightly or mismatched pots, and they are a novel way to gift wrap a plant for a friend. The container shown here is the basic form with a simple burlap flower decoration, but you can add a ribbon, a jute carry-handle, or long lengths of plaited jute to make a hanging container. For smaller or larger plant pots, adjust the quantity of burlap required. When watering the plant it is best to first remove the potted plant from the burlap container.

> CRAFT MIX AND MATCH
  Flower (page 20)
  Stenciling (page 114)
  Dyeing burlap (page 124)
  Bleaching burlap (page 126)

You will need

- Plant pot (preferably empty), 3½ inches (9 cm) high and 4 inches (10 cm) in diameter
- Burlap, 7 x 20 inches (18 x 51 cm), prewashed if required
- White glue and paintbrush
- Dressmaking pins
- Scissors
- Sewing machine and sewing thread
- Burlap to make a decorative flower (page 21)(optional)
- Sewing needle and thread (optional)

How to make the plant pot container

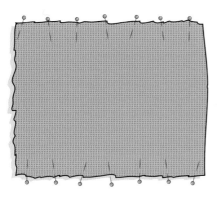

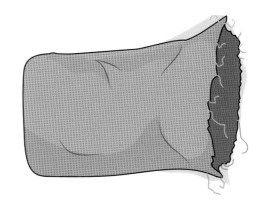

1 Coat the edges of the burlap with glue to prevent fraying. Fold the burlap in half, wrong side facing out, to make a rectangle 7 x 10 inches (18 x 25.5 cm). Pin the long sides together. Sew the pinned sides with a ¼ inch (6 mm) seam. Sew each seam twice.

2 Turn the burlap inside out. Lower the plant pot into the burlap container—the base of the pot sits on the bottom of the bag.

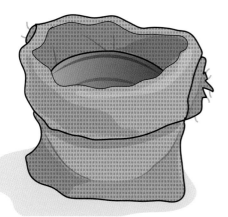

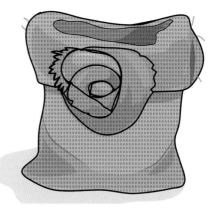

3 Fold the opened top end of the container over a few times to form a collar that sits above the top of the plant pot.

4 Follow the steps for the flower on page 21. Stitch or glue the flower to the burlap container with needle and thread.

Tote bag

Making your own reusable bag for life is incredibly easy! Burlap is perfect for creating a practical, strong, washable, and very eco-friendly bag for shopping, exercise gear, work, and more. This tote measures roughly 13 inches (33 cm) square. I made the tote using a burlap sack—the stenciled labels were too good to hide—and the handles were made from a woven belt, but burlap ribbon, an old necktie, leather, denim, or macramé will also work well.

> CRAFT MIX AND MATCH
  Stenciling (page 116)
  Stamping (page 118)
  Felt appliqué (page 132)

You will need

- Burlap, 14 x 30 inches (35.5 x 76 cm), prewashed if required
- Woven belt or similar, two pieces 2 x 12 inches (5 x 30.5 cm)
- Iron and ironing surface
- Dressmaking pins
- Sewing machine and thread
- Felt, burlap, or other fabric for the pocket, about 8 x 6 inches (20.5 x 15 cm), but allow more if the fabric needs to be hemmed
- Scissors

How to make the tote bag

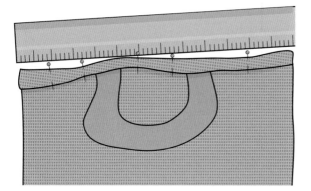

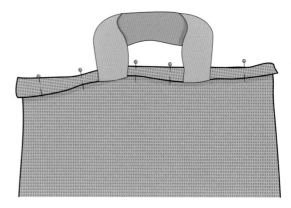

1 To the wrong side of the burlap, fold both short sides 1 inch (2.5 cm), pin, and iron flat. Insert the ends of one handle under the fold, 4 inches (10 cm) in from both long sides, and pushing the handle ends right into the pressed folds. Insert the other handle into the other short side in the same manner.

2 Fold the handles back over the folds and pin in place. Sew the short sides, sewing the sections where the handles are inserted twice. If you are stenciling or adding other decoration to the burlap, do it now before the pocket and long sides are stitched.

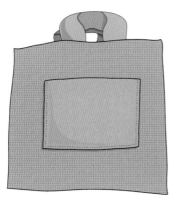

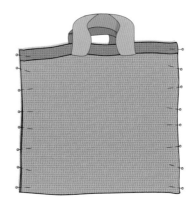

3 To add the pocket, fold the burlap in half, right side out, handles and sides aligned. Work out the best position for the pocket, and then pin in place through only one layer of the burlap. (Hem pocket if necessary before sewing to the tote.) Unfold burlap, and sew pocket along three sides, leaving the top open.

4 Fold the burlap in half, wrong side out, aligning handles and edges. Pin the long sides and sew, starting at the fold and working toward the opening. Turn the tote inside out and trim threads.

Curtain

This single drop burlap curtain is a simple home décor addition that can be cut and sewn in an afternoon. It has tab tops, but you can also use drapery rings. You can buy burlap from a fabric store or repurpose burlap sacks. The first thing to do is take accurate measurements of the window. If using burlap sacks, unpick the seams and line up open bags to get the width and length of fabric that you need. Keep measuring the curtain as you work. A curtain that gapes at the bottom is not pretty!

You will need

- Burlap, window measurements plus 2 inches (5 cm) to width and 8 inches (20.5 cm) to length; and if using burlap sack, window measurements plus ¼ inch (6 mm) for each joining seam, 2 inches (5 cm) in width and 8 inches (20.5 cm) in length, prewashed and ironed

- Tape measure and chalk

- Scissors

- Lace-edged burlap garland or similar for the tab tops, cut to 8-inch (20.5-cm) lengths, and allowing one tab for every 10 inches (25.5 cm) of curtain width

- Dressmaking pins

- Material for tieback 20 inches (51 cm) by 4 inches (10 cm)

How to make the curtain

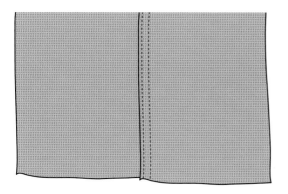

1 If using burlap sacks, join sacks together to make a panel of the correct width and length including hem and seam allowances. Burlap and burlap sacks: cut a straight edge for the top edge of the curtain.

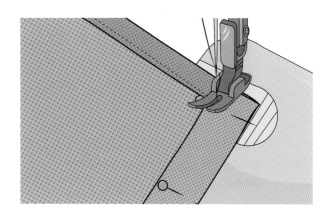

2 Burlap: fold over both vertical edges ½ inch (1.5 cm). Fold again ½ inch (1.5 cm) and then pin, iron, and sew. Fold and pin top edge over ½ inch (1.5 cm) and iron. Remove pins, fold again 1½ inches (4 cm), and pin and iron. Sew this hem 1¼ inches (3 cm) from the top edge. Burlap sacks: blanket-stitch (page 120) both vertical edges. Follow instructions above to hem the top edge.

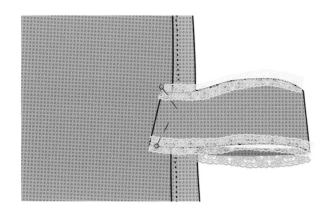

3 To make tab tops: fold and iron both short ends of each tab top over ½ inch (1.5 cm) to the wrong side. Mark tab top positions (evenly spaced) along the top of the curtain with chalk. Pin tab tops to the curtain (as shown), and machine- or hand-sew to the curtain. Hang the curtain from the pole.

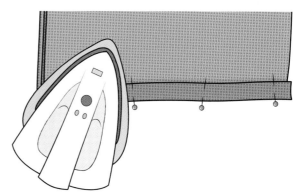

4 Burlap and burlap sacks: fold and pin the bottom hem so that the length is perfect. Remove the curtain from the pole. Burlap: fold the bottom edge of curtain twice to make a double hem following the pinned turn, and iron. Rehang the curtain, check length, and then sew the hem. Burlap sacks: cut a straight edge along the bottom of the curtain following your pinned turn. Blanket-stitch this edge.

Cushion cover

There are so many ways to make a cushion cover. My favorite method is the envelope technique because it dispenses with the need to fit a fiddly zipper. You just measure, cut, and stitch. Leave the burlap in its natural state or dye it and add felt appliqué, stencils, or a stamped pattern. If you are not recovering an old cushion, you can buy cushion forms at fabric and craft stores.

> CRAFT MIX AND MATCH
   Decorative edge stitch (page 120)
   Dyeing burlap (page 124)
   Felt appliqué (page 134)

You will need

- Burlap, twice the size of the cushion plus generous seam and hem allowances, and prewashed if required
- Old cushion or cushion form
- Ruler and chalk
- Scissors
- Dressmaking pins
- Felt in four colors
- Sewing machine and thread

How to make the cushion cover

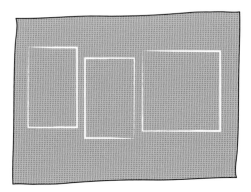

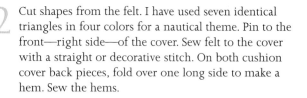

1 For the cushion cover front: measure the cushion form and add 1 inch (2.5 cm) to the width and length for seam allowances, and mark this out on the burlap. For the cushion cover back: two pieces that are each a cushion width plus 1 inch (2.5 cm) seam allowance wide by two-thirds of the cushion length. (If the cushion is 12 x 15 inches (30.5 x 38 cm), each back piece will measure 13 x 10 inches (33 x 25.5 cm).)

2 Cut shapes from the felt. I have used seven identical triangles in four colors for a nautical theme. Pin to the front—right side—of the cover. Sew felt to the cover with a straight or decorative stitch. On both cushion cover back pieces, fold over one long side to make a hem. Sew the hems.

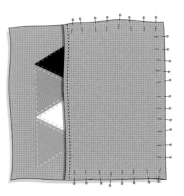

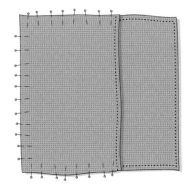

3 Lay the cover front, right side up. Lay one back piece on top, right side down, hemmed edge to the left, and right edges aligned, as shown. Pin the edges. Lay the remaining back piece, right side down, hemmed edge to the right, and left edge aligned with the cover front. This piece will partially overlap the other back piece. Pin together around outside edges only.

4 Sew pinned sides together, ½ inch (1.5 cm) in from the edges. (If you want a loose fit, then sew ¼ inch/ 6 mm in from the edges.) Turn the cover inside out, push the corners out, and insert the cushion form into the cover.

Boutonnière

This boutonnière, or buttonhole decoration, is a modern take on the old-fashioned rose or carnation. It will survive a long day unblemished and unwilted, and it makes the perfect keepsake to remember a very special occasion. You can customize one for each member of a wedding party, for example. Add some whimsy—something old, something new, something blue—by repurposing old buttons or jewelry, and swapping fabric flowers for dried ones. The possibilities are endless!

> CRAFT MIX AND MATCH
> Stenciling (page 116)
> Decorative edge stitch (page 120)
> Dyeing burlap (page 124)

You will need

- Cardstock
- Plain burlap, one piece 2 x 4 inches (5 x 10 cm) and a strip ½ x 6 inches (1.5 x 15 cm); and colored burlap, 2 x 4 inches (5 x 10 cm) for each boutonnière
- White glue and paintbrush or glue gun and glue sticks
- Chalk
- Brooch backing or safety pin
- Fabric or dried flowers and old jewelry or buttons
- Scissors
- Clothespins

How to make the boutonnière

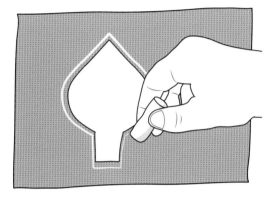

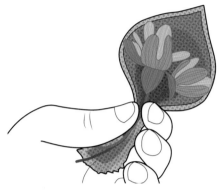

1 Brush plain burlap all over one side with white glue to help prevent fraying. While the glue dries, draw a leaf, no larger than the fabric, onto cardstock. Lay the template onto the plain burlap once dry, trace around it with chalk, and cut it out. Repeat for the colored burlap. Lay the colored leaf on top of the plain leaf.

2 Lay flowers and leaves onto the burlap leaves, the flowers sitting in the center with the stems resting on the burlap "stem." Dab glue onto the burlap stem. Enclose the flower stems inside and use clothespins to hold everything in place while the glue dries.

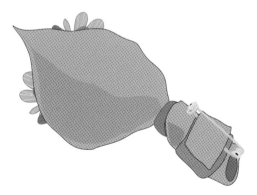

3 Dab the one end of the strip of burlap with glue and press this to the top of the stem. Wrap the strip twice around the stem.

4 Position the back plate of the opened brooch pin onto the back of the stem. Wind the burlap strip around the stem and the backing plate, adding glue when necessary. Make sure glue doesn't get into the mechanism of the brooch. Leave to dry before pinning the boutonnière onto clothing.

Table runner

A burlap table runner is equally at home on a dinner table for a formal soirée or potluck gathering, or on a rustic garden table for an *al fresco* party. Keep the runner *au naturel* or embellish with stenciling, stamping, painting, or embroidery. Tassels would also look really good along the two short edges. I kept mine super simple, letting the texture of the vintage burlap and colored stripes do all the talking.

The first task is to measure your table. A table runner is approximately one-third the width of the table, and 18–24 inches (45.5–61 cm) longer than the length of the table so that the runner drapes over the two short ends of the table.

You will need

- Long metal rule and chalk
- Burlap (for quantity guideline see above), prewashed and ironed
- Scissors
- Fusible webbing, 1-inch (2.5-cm) wide and long enough to trim to all four edges of the runner
- Dressmaking pins
- Ribbon, 1-inch (2.5-cm) wide and long enough to apply to all four edges of the runner
- Iron and ironing board
- Cotton cloth

How to make the table runner

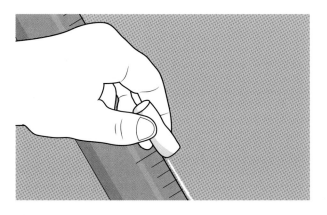

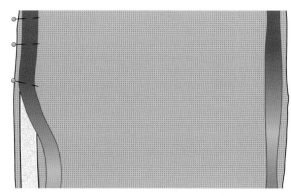

1 Use the chalk to transfer your runner measurements to the burlap. Cut out the runner. Note: if using a burlap sack for your runner as I did, unpick the long side seams, but do not cut off the hem on the short sides. Retaining this hem will prevent the burlap fraying.

2 Pin the fusible webbing along all four edges on the wrong side of the runner. Pin the ribbon on top of the fusible webbing.

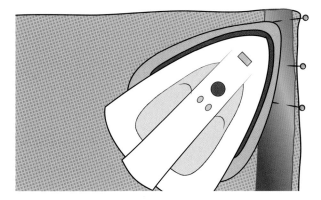

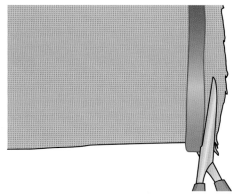

3 Set your iron to a high heat, but do not use the steam setting. Lay one end of runner on the ironing surface, ribbon side facing up. You may need to cover the ribbon with a cotton cloth to prevent damaging it. Follow ironing instructions on the webbing packaging.

4 When the ironing is complete and the ribbon is bonded to the burlap, trim any straggly threads of burlap and neaten edges with scissors. You can now decorate your runner as you want.

Apron

Here's the perfectly practical accessory for days of gardening chores or afternoons of barbecue joy—a burlap bib apron. Though a practical cover-up, it does not lack in style with its contrast trim. If you like, design, cut, and sew pockets for the apron that best meet your needs. Get a pattern for your apron by tracing around an old apron onto a large piece of paper. The apron in this project measures approximately 28 x 22 inches (70 x 56 cm) If you want to make adjustments to width or length, make these adjustments to your pattern. Amend these steps to make a half apron or even a tabard.

You will need

- ¾–1 square yard (0.75–1 sq m) burlap
- Old apron (optional)
- Large piece of paper and pencil
- Scissors
- Dressmaking pins
- Chalk
- 1–2 rolls of 2-inch (5-cm) canvas or a grosgrain ribbon
- 1–2 rolls of fusible webbing 2 inches (5 cm) wide
- Sewing machine and thread

How to make the apron

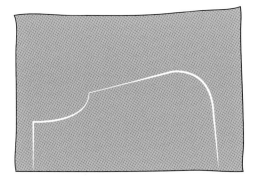

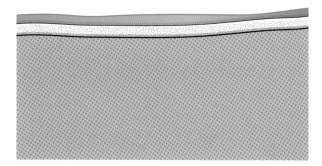

1 Cut out your pattern and fold in half widthwise. Fold the burlap in half and pin the folded edge of the pattern along the folded edge of the burlap. Trace around the pattern with chalk. Remove pins and pattern. Cut out the apron.

2 Lay the ribbon, about 8 feet (2.5 m), wrong side up, on your work surface. Lay the webbing on the ribbon. Fold and pin the ribbon and webbing—webbing on the inside—to midway (waist level) on the left edge of the apron, down and around the bottom, and up the right edge to the midway position. Repeat for the top edge of the apron. Iron the webbing and ribbon and trim ends to line up with the burlap.

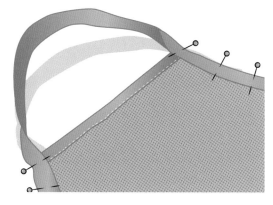

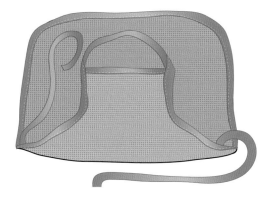

3 Run out enough ribbon to trim the left and right edges from the midpoints upward, to make two apron ties—24 inches (60 cm) is usual per tie—and to make the loop that goes around the neck. Pin the ribbon in position, inserting webbing where the ribbon is trimming the burlap. Fold the ribbon and webbing around the burlap. Try on the apron, check the fit, and make any necessary adjustments before starting step 4.

4 Iron the webbing and ribbon. Sew a ¼ inch (6 mm) seam around all sides of the apron to further secure the ribbon trim. Finish your apron by adding pockets or decoration.

Coffee cup sleeve

A burlap coffee cup sleeve is the perfect way to make that cup-of-joe from your favorite takeout purveyor truly your own! Once you have made your first coffee sleeve, you can incorporate different materials or adjust the dimensions to suit other types of containers. Soon, you'll be making one for all your friends!

> CRAFT MIX AND MATCH
> Stenciling (page 116)
> Decorative edge stitch (page 120)
> Dyeing burlap (page 124)

You will need

- Cardboard coffee sleeve from your favorite takeout
- Scrap fabric or felt (the thicker the better to provide protection from hot contents)
- Chalk
- Scissors
- Burlap, about 3 x 12 inches (7.5 x 30.5 cm)
- Fabric glue
- Clothespins
- Felt
- Embroidery needle and floss or sewing machine and thread
- 2 buttons, about 1 inch (2.5 cm) in diameter, or 3–4 smaller buttons

How to make the coffee cup sleeve

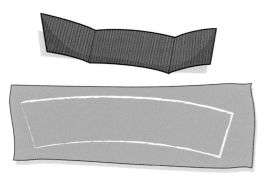

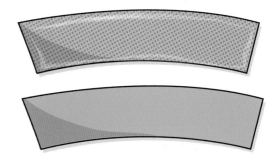

1 Carefully pull apart the seam on the cardboard sleeve to use as the template for your coffee cup sleeve. Lay it flat on top of the fabric or felt and trace around it in chalk and add an extra 1 inch (2.5 cm) to the length. (This is so the ends overlap.) Cut it out. Lay the pattern onto the burlap, trace around it, adding the extra 1 inch (2.5 cm) to the length, and cut it out.

2 Apply fabric glue to the four edges of the wrong side of the burlap. Press and smooth the felt onto the glued side of burlap, aligning all edges. Use clothespins to hold the burlap and felt together while the glue dries.

3 When the glue is dry, decorate the outside of the sleeve. Cut out felt shapes and glue to the sleeve with fabric glue. Apply further decoration.

4 Sew a decorative edge stitch on all edges. Overlap the ends of the sleeve (check the fit on the coffee cup) and pin together. Hand- or machine-sew the seam. Position buttons on the overlap and attach by sewing through all the layers of fabric. Knot ends and trim.

Hemp
& Jute

Overview

Hemp and jute are natural fibers that are strong, durable, and perfect for crafting! They can be used for macramé, knitting, crocheting, and stitching, and which of the two you select for a project is mostly down to your own personal preference.

From experience, though, I would recommend hemp for macramé jewelry, and jute for a macramé hanger. While both are very durable, hemp is denser and stronger and much softer than jute, which can be a little scratchy for a bracelet or anything coming in contact with skin.

Hemp cord originates from the cannabis plant. The main uses of hemp fiber are in rope, sacking, carpet, nets, and webbing. Hemp fiber is stronger yet softer than materials like cotton, lasts twice as long, and is not affected by mildew. You will find hemp in local craft and dollar stores. If you want a large roll of hemp or dyed hemp, then definitely head to a craft store or online supplier. Hemp is available in a few thicknesses.

Jute comes from the stem and ribbon (outer skin) of the jute plant. Jute is used for twine, rope, and burlap. It's affordable and easy to find in craft, dollar, or hardware stores. Jute is available in lots of colors and thicknesses.

If using hemp or jute for stitching, you'll want to pick up a darning needle with a large eye. Both fibers can be used for any project utilizing burlap—they are a perfect trio of natural materials.

Feel free to experiment with these materials by dyeing them using a normal fabric dye or one that incorporates food coloring. Always do a dye test before taking the plunge on a whole roll of hemp or jute.

My favorite projects—and dare I say my latest DIY addiction—are anything involving macramé. There is just something so therapeutic in making knots that magically grow into a chain of loveliness. A simple glass container can inexpensively become a hanging planter or vase filled with succulents or flowers in a jiffy. Repurposing beads from a thrift store along with a length of hemp soon becomes a bracelet. Once you get into macramé, there's no limit to what you can create.

Lampshade

Here's an easy way to restyle an old lampshade. All you need is jute, a glue gun, and a bit of time, but it is worth the effort. Choose a simple lampshade without curves to save yourself time and frustration. Once you have updated the shade, you can set about refurbishing the base to match. The quantity of jute required will depend on the size of the shade, but a roll of jute should be more than adequate. This project requires lots of glue, so check you have plenty to hand.

> CRAFT MIX AND MATCH
> Flower (page 20)
> Knotting and beading (page 130)

You will need

- Lampshade
- Roll of jute
- 15 feet (4.5 m) of ¼-inch (6-mm) rope is sufficient for a shade 8 inches (20 cm) in diameter
- Glue gun and glue sticks
- White glue and paintbrush
- Scissors

How to make the lampshade

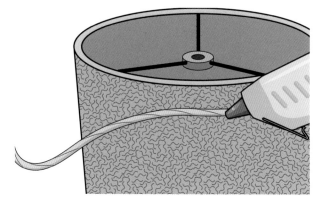

1. Remove the lampshade from the base and remove or cut off tassels, trim, and decoration. Dust or vacuum the shade and then wipe the shade with a damp cloth. Using the glue gun, glue the free end of the jute to the top of the shade about 1 inch (2.5 cm) below the top edge. (The rope will be used to trim the top and bottom of the lampshade.)

2. Dab glue onto the lampshade and then press the jute into it as you work your way around the shade. Ideally, one continuous piece of jute should be used rather than multiple pieces. Keep dabbing on the glue and wrapping the jute until you reach the bottom of the shade. Don't forget to leave 1 inch (2.5 cm) for the rope trim. Trim and glue the end of the jute.

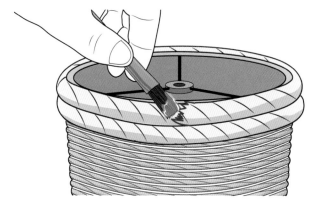

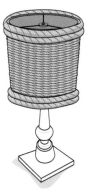

3. Dip one end of the rope into the white glue to prevent fraying and allow to dry before gluing and wrapping the rope around the top of the lampshade. Trim end, dab with glue to prevent fraying, and glue to the shade.

4. Repeat step 3 to add the rope trim to the bottom of the lampshade. Allow to dry before adding any other decoration or fixing to the base. This shade will create a textured and subdued light.

Beaded macramé bracelet

Hemp bracelets are fun gifts for friends and something they can wear for years. They can also double as pretty summer anklets. Raid your own stash of beads or buy beaded necklaces from thrift stores. Check that the hole in the beads will be large enough to accommodate two thicknesses of hemp. Once you've made one of these bracelets, experiment with other macramé patterns, more intricate beading, and fancy clasps. To help you make the bracelet, we've colored the cords red and blue in the step illustrations.

You will need

- Clipboard or board with nail
- 2 pieces of hemp, 60–62 inches (152–158 cm) in length
- 5–6 beads, at least ½ inch (1.5 cm) in diameter with a large center hole
- Scissors

How to make the beaded macramé bracelet

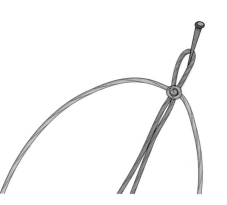

1 Fold one length of hemp in half, and secure the loop to the clipboard or nail. Lay the midpoint of the second length of hemp under the first, about ¾ inch (2 cm) down from the nail, and tie a single overhand knot.

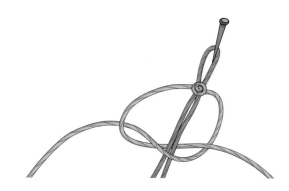

2 Thread the left blue cord under the red cords, and over the right blue cord. Lay the right blue cord over the red cords and under the left blue cord. Pull to set the knot. Repeat this square knot for 2 inches (5 cm), alternately reversing which cord goes over and which goes under the other cords.

3 Thread a bead onto the red cords, pushing it up to the base of the square knots. Repeat step 2 four more times, tying square knots for 1 inch (2.5 cm) and threading on the second, third, fourth, and fifth beads. Tie square knots for a further 1 inch (2.5 cm).

4 To finish the bracelet: tie two single knots in the four cords. To wear the bracelet: lay the bracelet over the wrist, and thread the double knot through the loop at the other end of the bracelet. If loose, tie another single knot. Trim the ends.

Rope frame

Add a quirky, almost nautical, feature to your décor with a hemp-edged mirror, photo, or pinboard frame. This clever upcycling trick works best on a frame of molded wood. Frames like this can be found in thrift and secondhand stores. You may need to paint or distress the frame's existing finish before beginning this project. A glue gun will make light, quick work of securing the hemp.

You will need

- Hemp, about ¼-inch (6-mm) wide and sufficent to go around the frame at least five times depending on the width of the frame
- Wood molded frame
- Glue gun and glue sticks or white glue and paintbrush
- Scissors

How to make the rope frame

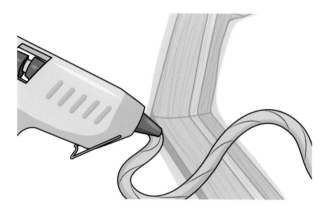

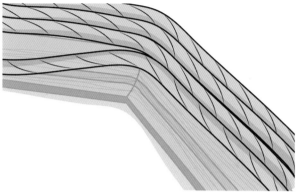

1. Remove the mirror or picture from the frame. Clean the frame if needed. Warm up the glue gun. Glue the free end of the hemp to the outside edge of the frame.

2. Slowly and carefully cover the frame with the hemp, dabbing glue onto the frame to secure the hemp. When you have gone around the frame once and are back to where you started, continue working inward, applying glue and laying the hemp into position.

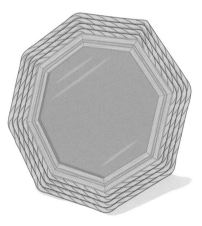

Finishing touch

If nautical is not your thing, look out for laser-cut wooden decorations in craft stores. There are so many to choose from: teapots, boots, suns and moons, gardening tools, animals, and more. The laser-cut is simply glued to the hemp. What could be easier?

3. Make sure the rows of hemp lay closely together and are as neat as possible. Keep gluing and adding the hemp until the frame is covered. Replace the mirror or picture back into the frame.

Coaster

There's nothing you cannot do, make, or craft if you have a trusty glue gun. In this project, the glue gun makes light work of updating a plain or old cork coaster or trivet with hemp coiled into a tight spiral. A word of advice: choose circular, rather than square or rectangular coasters or trivets. If you fancy brightening up your tableware, use colored hemp. You'll find a collection of wonderful colors in craft stores or online.

> CRAFT MIX AND MATCH
> Stenciling (page 116)
> Stamping (page 118)
> Decorative edge stitch (page 120)

You will need

- Cork coaster or trivet 4 inches (10 cm) in diameter
- Craft knife
- A roll of ³⁄₈-inch (9-mm) hemp
- Small screwdriver
- Glue gun and glue sticks, or white glue in a tube with a fine nozzle
- Scissors

How to make the coaster

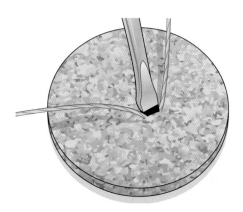

1 Measure and mark the dead center of the coaster. Cut a shallow slit ¼ inch (1.5 cm) in length over the center point. If using a glue gun, now is the time to warm it up ready for use.

2 Use the screwdriver to push the free end of the hemp into the slit.

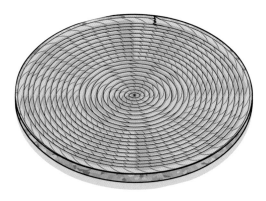

3 Secure the hemp into the slit with a dab of glue. Allow to dry. Coil the hemp around the center, adding dabs of glue to keep the hemp in place. Make sure the coils lay neatly alongside each other rather than overlapping or being gappy.

4 Continue coiling the hemp to make a seemingly endless spiral. When the spiral reaches the edge, trim the hemp and tuck the end under the coil. Glue in position. Leave to dry.

Braided headphone wrap

Add personality to your headphones using braided hemp, plain or colored, and beads upcycled from broken or out-of-fashion jewelry. Braiding the hemp is easier if the jack end of the cable is taped to a work surface or gripped by the clamp on a clipboard. To manage the long lengths of hemp needed, coil each length—leaving enough to work with—and secure with a rubberband. Release more cord when required. If you run out of cord at any point, tape the last inch of cord to the cable and then knot another length of cord to the cable just below the last knot. As you tie more knots, the tape will be covered and the loose end of cord made secure.

You will need

- Adhesive tape or a clipboard
- Hemp 70 feet (22 m) in length or about four times the length of your headphones
- Scissors
- 50–60 small beads
- White glue and a small paintbrush
- Clothespin

How to make the braided headphone wrap

1   Tape or clamp the jack end of the headphones to a flat surface. We will braid this section first, and then braid the thinner cables that lead to the headphone buds. Knot the midpoint of the hemp to the top of the cable, just below the jack.

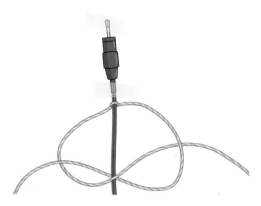

2   Thread the right cord under the cable and over the left cord. Thread the left cord over the cable, up through the D-shape on the right and over the right cord. Pull to set the first knot. Repeat this knot, threading a bead onto the right cord every inch (2.5 cm) or so. Note: the braid twists to create a spiral, so you may want to reverse which cord goes under and over the other cords to keep the braid straight.

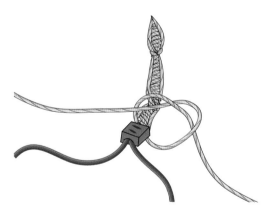

3   When you reach the point where the cable splits into two thinner cables, knot the cords around the cable securely and trim ends. Dab the knot with glue, and clamp with a clothespin until the glue is dry.

4   Untape or unclamp the jack end and tape or clamp the left ear bud to the work surface. Braid this cable following steps 1–3. When you reach the top (where the cable splits), knot the cords, trim ends, dab with glue, and clamp in a clothespin. Repeat steps 1–4 for the right ear bud.

Decorated vase

Upcycle a glass container that has been salvaged from your recycle bin or give an old vase or thrift store bargain a second life using jute and scrap fabric. Once you have created your first vase and mastered the technique, you will see how easy it is to create something wonderful and perfect for your home without breaking the bank! A word of advice: start with a uniformly shaped container to make fitting the fabric sleeve easier.

> CRAFT MIX AND MATCH
> Flower (page 20)

You will need

- Glass container or bottle
- Glue gun and glue sticks
- 1–2 rolls of jute, depending on the size of the container
- Piece of scrap fabric, sufficient to wrap around the container
- Scissors
- Dressmaking pins
- Fabric glue
- Clothespins
- Rubberbands
- Burlap (optional)
- Rope or cord (optional)

How to make the decorated vase

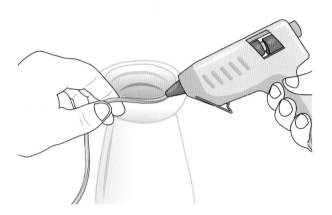

1 Clean the container and plug in the glue gun. Once the glue gun is warmed, dab glue around the top of the container and press the free end of the jute into it. Keep dabbing on more glue while wrapping the jute neatly around the container. Wrap the entire container, then trim and glue the end in place. Leave to dry.

2 Wrap the fabric around the container and fold the fabric to get it the correct width and height. Mark with pins and remove from the container. Trim fabric (if necessary), then on both long sides and one short side fold and pin to the wrong side. Recheck that the fabric fits around the container. When satisfied, iron the folds and remove the pins.

3 Apply the fabric glue to the inside of the three folded edges. Press firmly on the glue to secure contact, and then use clothespins to clamp the folds. Leave to dry.

4 When the glue is dry, apply fabric glue to the wrong side of the fabric. Wrap the fabric around the container and secure with rubberbands while the glue dries. Add further decoration like a hemp trim, which can sit above and/or below the fabric, or a bouquet of burlap flowers.

Macramé hanging vase

Macramé is surprisingly addictive, almost therapeutic once you've mastered the technique. A round vase is cradled by a web of knotted jute cords, which is suspended by long cords from a ceiling or shelf. In place of a vase use a preserving or jelly jar. As you gain confidence making the knots, it will free you up to get more creative and adventurous with beads and other items that you can knot into the cords. Keep a ruler handy to check measurements throughout the project, and don't tighten a knot until you're sure it's in the right place.

You will need

- Working board and nail
- Wooden ring 2 inches (5 cm) in diameter
- 3 pieces of jute, each 50 inches (127 cm) in length will make a hanger 15 inches (38 cm) long and suitable for a vase 6 x 6 inches (15 x 15 cm)
- 2–3 large beads with a center hole no smaller than ¼ inch (6 mm) in diameter
- Ruler
- Scissors
- Round glass vase or similar container

How to make the macramé hanging vase

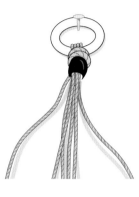

1 Clamp or tie the ring to a clipboard or to a nail on a piece of board. Align the ends of the three lengths of jute and find the midpoint. Thread the midpoint loop through the ring, and then thread all six ends of the jute through the loop. Pull to set the lark's head knot against the ring. Thread the six ends into a bead and push the bead up to the knot. Secure the bead with a knot.

2 Using one cord on the left and one on the right as the working cords, tie a square knot (page 131) on the filler cords (the four cords in the center). Pull on the knot to tighten, and then tie more square knots for 1 inch (2.5 cm).

3 Separate the cords into three groups of two. Tie a double knot onto each pair of cords 8 inches (20.5 cm) down from the last square knot. Pair the cords again, but with different partners. Tie a double knot in each new pair 4 inches (10 cm) down from the previous knot.

4 Knot all six cords together 1–2-inches (2.5–5 cm) down from the last knot. Tie square knots, using one cord on the left and one on the right, for 1 inch (2.5 cm). Thread a bead onto the six cords and push it up to the square knot. Tie a double knot under the bead. Trim the cord ends 4 inches (10 cm) from the bead. Place the vase in the web of cords and suspend the hanger from a secure hook.

Floor rug

This organically shaped, stepping stone-like rug is made of jute coils of various size, texture, and color. The finished look is so wonderful it could be used as wall art, embellished as suggested in the Craft Mix and Match (below). In a scaled-down form the coils could become placemats, trivets, or a table decoration. It is a good idea to roughly sketch out your design for this floor rug first.

> CRAFT MIX AND MATCH
> Decorative edge stitch (page 120)
> Cross-stitch (page 122)
> Knotting and beading (page 130)
> Felt appliqué (page 134)

You will need

- Rolls of jute in various colors; to make one coil 9 inches (23 cm) in diameter, you will need 15 feet (4.5 m) of ¼-inch (6-mm) jute
- Glue gun and glue sticks or white glue and spongebrush
- Scissors
- Felt
- Long dressmaking pins
- Embroidery thread and needle
- Double-sided tape
- Anti-slip backing material

How to make the floor rug

1   Tie a knot in the free end of a roll of jute, and then start coiling jute around the knot. Dab glue onto the outer edge of the coil and press the jute to it. Continue coiling until you make a coil of the diameter you want.

2   Make more jute coils of different sizes and colors. Overlap the coils to create your design. Glue the overlapping sections of disks to the disks below. Allow to dry. (It may help to clothespin the disks while the glue dries.)

3   Place the coils onto the felt, right side up, and pin into position. Trim felt ½ inch (1.5 cm) from around the rug. Use the embroidery thread and needle to cross-stitch the coils to the felt.

4   Turn the rug so the right side is facing down. Generously cover the back of the rug with double-sided tape. Remove the protective backing from the tape and, section by section, smooth on the anti-slip material. Turn the rug over and trim the excess felt and anti-slip material from around the edges.

Coiled bowl

A jute bowl is a décor statement—especially if you make a collection of them in various sizes, shapes, and colors—and the ideal safe place for keys, loose change, cell phone, pens, and more. But it has one more unexpected use: as the "wrapping" for a small present it is the gift that keeps on giving in a very eco-friendly way. Once you have made one, experiment by adding handles and a leather or suede trim. Jute is available in varying thickness, but I recommend using the thickest you can find. It will make the project easier and quicker.

You will need

- Plastic bowl, or a ceramic one wrapped in waxed paper, 5 x 4 inches (12.5 x 10.5 cm) to use as the mold
- 15 feet (38 cm) jute $^3/_{16}$-inch (5-mm) wide
- Glue gun and glue sticks or white glue and paintbrush
- Clothespins
- Scissors

How to make the coiled bowl

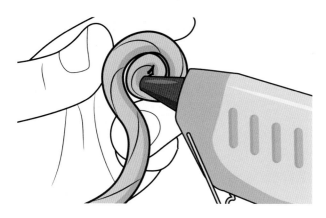

1 Fold one free end of the jute over 1 inch (2.5 cm). Dab the inside of the fold with glue and clothespin until the glue is dry.

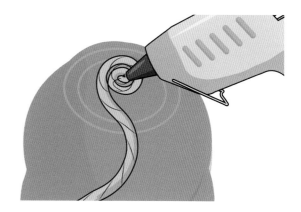

2 Position folded end in the center of the base of the mold. Coil jute around the center, dabbing glue onto the outside edge of the jute and pressing the next layer of cord to it. Do not glue the rope to the mold!

3 When the base is covered, start wrapping jute around the walls of the mold. Dab glue onto the trailing section of jute and press this to the already coiled jute.

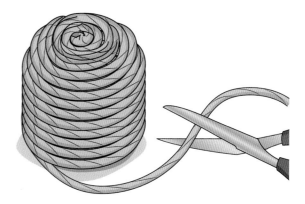

4 When you get to the lip of the mold, cut the rope and glue the end to the top of your bowl. Leave the bowl to dry, and then remove the mold. Decorate the bowl with some trim as in the photo opposite or leave it in its beautiful raw state.

Macramé bag

Macramé and jute are perfect partners-in-craft! Make a practical, simple, and reusable grocery bag using jute, and then customize and upcycle it with beads or glamorous repurposed jewelry. You will find everything you need at a craft store and in your own treasure box of useful things. This macramé bag is about 18 inches (45 cm) deep. Because this project is slightly more detailed than others featured in the book, we've featured more in-depth instructions on the following page.

Simple knotting is ideal for a summer tote. You can change the look of the bag using simple double knots to create the netting instead of square knots, or use Josephine knots for something more elegant. (You will find instructions for this knot on the Internet.) To add color or to introduce a different material, cut an old T-shirt into narrow strips and tie these into macramé, or use the strips in place of jute completely. There is nothing but creativity preventing you from incorporating beads or buttons into the knotting, or sewing them on when the bag is complete. Shells look wonderful and are perfect for a beach tote. You will find techniques for making a tiny hole in the shells on the Internet. Also experiment with the handles. When I've made this bag before I've used repurposed handles from thrift store finds, vintage handles from garage sales, and leather handles from an old belt. If you want to adjust the width of your bag, increase the number of cords you knot to each handle. To make the bag deeper, simply increase the length of the cords.

You will need

- Roll of 2- or 3-ply jute to cover the handles (quantity will depend on the size of the handles)
- Pair of wood or plastic bag handles
- White glue and paintbrush
- 20 pieces of 2- or 3-ply jute 6 feet (2 m) in length and one piece 3 feet (1 m) in length
- Clothes hanger
- 20 beads with center holes $1/8$-inch (3–4 mm) in diameter
- Darning needle

CRAFT MIX AND MATCH
Flower (page 20)
Dyeing burlap (page 124)
Knotting and beading (page 130)

How to make the macramé bag

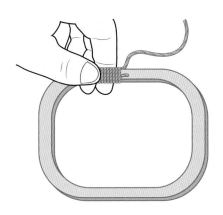

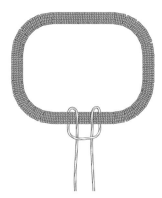

1   Using your roll of jute lay a 2-inch (5-cm) loop of the free end along the inside of one handle, and glue it in place. Wrap the jute around the handle, covering the loop. Cover the whole handle with close-set jute coils. Trim the jute and glue the end to the inside of the handle. Leave to dry. Repeat for the other handle.

2   Fold one 6-foot (2-m) length of jute in half. Thread the midpoint up through the center of one handle, over the handle to the back, and then thread the two free ends through the loop. Pull to set this lark's head knot. Repeat to attach nine more lengths of jute to this handle for a total of ten. Repeat to attach the remaining ten cords to the other handle.

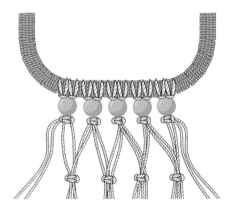

3   Separate the 20 cords into five groups of four cords. Thread a bead onto each group and tie two square knots (page 131) below each bead. Repeat for the other handle.

4   On one handle separate out two cords on the far left and on the far right, leaving you with 16 working cords. Separate these cords into four groups of four cords and, about 2 inches (5 cm) down from your last square knot, tie two more square knots. Repeat this on the second handle.

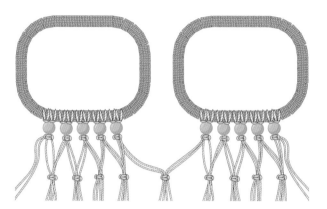

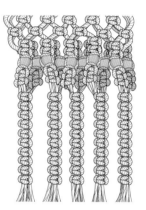

5 Hang your handles at opposite ends of a coat hanger so they face each other. Take the two set aside cords from the right of handle 1 and the left of handle 2 and bring them together to tie two square knots 4 inches (10 cm) down from your first knots. Repeat on the other side of the bag. Now starting at one end, separate out your cords into ten groups of four cords again and tie two more square knots 2 inches (5 cm) down from your last knots. Regroup your cords for the second row of knots as before and tie two square knots again.

6 Repeat this process until you have ten rows. When you have finished tying your rows, tie two square knots at the bottom of each group, thread on a bead and then tie two further square knots. Then bring two groups of cords together and secure these with a series of ten square knots. Repeat for the remaining groups of cords around the bag.

TIP

From step 3 onward, hang the handles 6–8 inches (15–20 cm) apart on a clothes hanger. Suspend the hanger from something secure at a good working height. This will let you work both sides of the bag and will make joining the sides much easier.

7 Cut a 3-foot (1-m) length of jute and knot it securely to one of the eight-cord groups. Combine all the cords together and wrap the jute tightly around the cords for 2 inches (5 cm). Thread the darning needle with the free end of the jute and use multiple stitches to secure the wrap to the bundle of cords. Tie off the jute with a double knot. Trim cords to neaten.

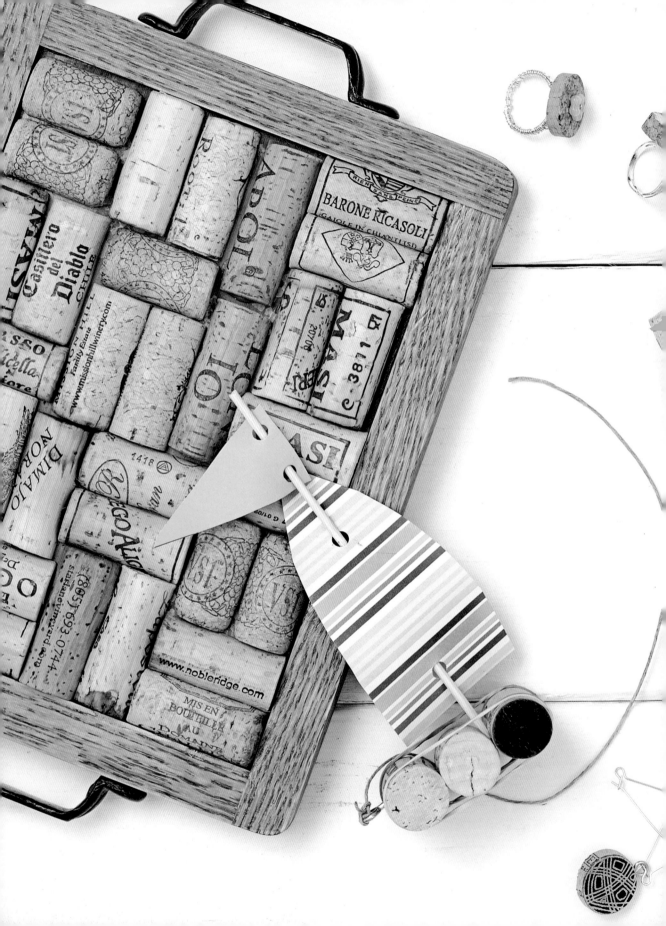

Overview

As far as crafting materials are concerned, cork is perfect for DIY-ing! It's sustainable, malleable, and easy to work with: plus it's cost effective. Cork is a buoyant, light colored material acquired from the outer layer of the bark from a cork oak.

Cork is an environmentally friendly material, as cork production is considered sustainable due to the fact that the cork is harvested from trees that continue to live, grow, and produce more cork for future harvests. It is in the commercial interest of the growers to keep their trees in fine health.

You can purchase cork strips, dots, sheets, and rolls in varying quantities and thicknesses from craft and hardware stores, and kitchen and dollar stores will stock cork stoppers if you cannot get your hands on enough wine corks. But if you want to make a sustainable statement, then prowl charity and thrift shops for pinboards, coasters, and other cork items that can be repurposed or upcycled; and for wine corks, look no further than your recycling bin or to a friendly local bar or restaurant who can save their wine corks for you.

Cork is an easy material to cut with a craft knife, bread knife, small hand saw, or scissors (though scissors are best for thin sheets of cork or for trimming and neatening cork edges). When cutting or trimming cork, go slowly and carefully as cork can rip or tear. Use a cutting mat when slicing wine corks, and as an extra precaution use a pair of pliers to grip the cork while you are cutting.

My favorite cork projects are earrings, pinboards, coasters, and trays. This material lends itself to being stenciled, stamped, and painted with graphics, patterns, and lettering. Try experimenting with découpage—gluing and layering cut-out pictures onto the cork and finishing with a coat of diluted white glue. Sometimes it's fun to hide the fact that you're upcycling; other times you might want your sustainable credentials to be front and center. Just enjoy and I'm sure you'll get addicted to creating with cork!

Printing stamp

Here's a fun, easy, and addictive DIY project using repurposed wine corks. Cork stamps are perfect for adding your personal stamp and flare to stationery, wrapping paper, and notebooks. You can print your stamp onto paper, fabric, cork, wood, and almost anything! Two useful tips to keep in mind: keep the stamp design simple so that carving it out is easy, and rinse the stamp regularly during use to keep detail and edges sharp and crisp.

> CRAFT MIX AND MATCH
Tote bag (page 24)
Cushion cover (page 28)
Wine bag (page 104)

You will need

- 1 wine cork per stamp
- Pen or pencil
- Craft knife
- Cutting mat
- Craft paints or inkpad

How to make the printing stamp

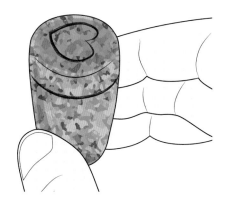

1 Draw your design onto the flattest end of the cork. The larger the design, the less cork that will need to be cut away. Draw a line around the neck of the cork about a ¼ inch (6 mm) down from the end on which you have drawn your design.

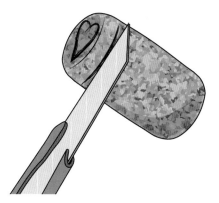

2 Slowly cut into the line around the neck of the cork. Keep in mind that the depth of your cutting should align with the contours of the design on the top of the cork. It is better to cut shallow, than too deep.

3 Cut vertically into your design following the outline you have drawn. Keep slicing away at the cork in both directions until the vertical cuts intersect with the horizontal cuts and pieces of cork fall away to leave the stamp standing proud on the top of the cork.

4 Carefully trim any unwanted notches or uneven edges. Press the stamp into the paint or ink pad, and get stamping! Always test the stamp on a scrap of your project medium before starting on your craft item.

Tray

Who would have guessed that a wine cork tray could be so easy to make yet look so good! The only tricky bit is slicing the corks in half along their length. For the actual tray, upcycle an unwanted tray (often found in thrift and charity stores) or purchase one from dollar or craft stores. I used an old picture frame, which had a secure plywood backing, and attached a pair of secondhand handles. I'm a reuser and lover of old items, so feel free to modify the project to include new items versus secondhand. Mounted on a wall, this tray could become a pinboard for reminders and photos.

You will need

- Wine corks: for a tray 12 x 16 inches (30.5 x 40.5 cm), you would need about 20 corks, halved

- Craft knife, bread knife, hand saw, or hacksaw

- Cutting mat

- Pliers (optional)

- Scissors

- Tray or picture frame

- Glue gun and glue sticks or glue appropriate to bonding cork to the tray surface

- Waterproof sealer or varnish (optional)

How to make the tray

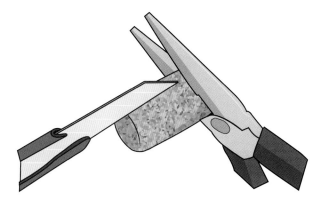

1 Wash the corks and leave to dry. Cut each cork lengthwise in half, making sure each half is the same size. This is the most time-consuming part with the highest probability of error. Take your time and be careful.

2 If attaching handles to the tray, you should do it now while there is access to the inside of the tray. Lay the halved corks in the tray, flat side down, and work out how you want to arrange them to make an interesting pattern and to fill the tray to the edges. Some corks may need further cutting so they fit snugly.

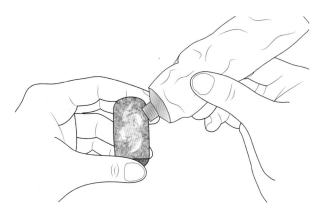

3 Leave the corks in place in the tray, removing one cork at a time to be glued. I found it helpful to start in one corner and work across to the opposite corner. Press each cork firmly in place, butting to adjoining corks.

4 Leave to dry thoroughly. Add your mark by painting, stamping, or stenciling the exterior of the tray. A wood tray might benefit from a coat of waterproof sealer or varnish.

Birdhouse

Here's a project for the whole family—a funky birdhouse made with wine corks, balsa or plywood, and dowel. The more corks you have, the bigger the mansion for your feathered friends. There is total freedom when it comes to detailing the house with doors, windows, stepping stones, and more. With a little bit of imagination you should find everything you need in your recycle bin. The quantities (as right) were sufficient for a birdhouse 8 x 8 x 9 inches (20.3 x 20.3 x 22.9 cm). A craft store will sell balsa project kits that are perfect for this DIY. I recommend that you use a glue gun for this project.

You will need

- For base: balsa sheet 8 x 9 inches (20.5 x 23 cm)
- To strengthen the base: 4 balsa sticks approximately ½ x ½ x 8 inches (1.5 x 1.5 x 20.5 cm)
- Glue gun and glue sticks
- Wood glue and paintbrush
- Clothespins
- For wall foundations: 2 balsa sticks 3½ x ¾ inches (9 x 2 cm) and 2 balsa sticks 8 x ¾ inches (20.5 x 2 cm)
- For uprights: 4 balsa sticks ½ x ½ x 2½ inches (1.5 x 1.5 x 6.5 cm)
- For roof: 2 balsa sheets 5 x 6 inches (12.5 x 15 cm)
- For eaves: 4 balsa sticks, 6 x ½ x ½ inches (15 x 1.5 x 1.5 cm)
- Scissors
- Craft knife
- 50–60 wine corks for walls and roof pitch
- 30 wine corks cut into disks for roof tiles
- For perch: dowel 2-3 inches (5–7.5 cm) long

How to make the birdhouse

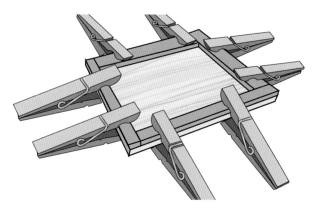

1 Lay the base on your work surface, and glue the four base strengthening sticks around the edge of the base using wood glue. Use clothespins to hold the balsa sheet and sticks in position while they dry. Note: strengthening sticks can be on the bottom, or visible on the top if you prefer.

2 Turn the birdhouse base over. To construct the house: glue the wall foundations to the base. Glue one end of each upright on each corner of the foundations. These posts will support the walls and the roof. When dry, start building the walls, joining each cork to the base, an upright, or to each other with the glue gun. Build the walls to the height of the uprights.

3 To make the roof: glue an eave stick to the short edges on the underside of each roof piece. Glue roof pieces on the house—you may need someone to hold these pieces—and glue corks along the ridge to support the pieces at the correct pitch. Note the position of the roof and eaves over the wall uprights. Hold the roof and corks in place until the glue dries.

4 Partially fill the space between the angled roof and the top of the front and back walls with glued corks. Tile the exterior of the roof with cork disks. Make a hole midway along the front wall with your craft knife and insert one end of the dowel to make the perch. Now, have fun adding details like a cork door to your birdhouse.

Drinks coaster

Why buy coasters when you can make your own! New cork sheeting is used for the upper surface while the base is made of plywood or damaged or stained coasters. Decorate the finished coasters with a stenciled design, cork stamp pattern, or freehand drawing. Alternatively you can simply use thicker cork sheeting.

> CRAFT MIX AND MATCH
> Stenciling (page 116)
> Stamping (page 118)

You will need

- Old coaster or plywood square roughly 4 x 4 x $^{3}/_{16}$ inches (10 x 10 x 0.5 cm)
- Wood glue
- $^{1}/_{8}$-inch (3 mm) thick cork sheet (a 22½ x 22½-inch/56 x 56-cm sheet is sufficient to make four coasters)
- Clothespins
- Craft knife
- Cutting mat
- Sandpaper
- Stencil
- Permanent marker or acrylic paint and paintbrush
- Waterproof sealer, varnish, or diluted white glue and paintbrush

How to make the drinks coaster

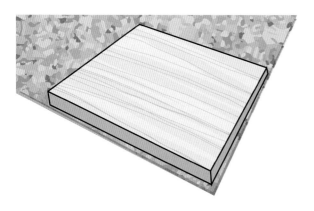

1   Sand the plywood smooth and ensure that the surface is clean and free of grease. Spread glue over the upper surface of the coaster and press it onto the back of the cork sheet, aligning two adjoining edges of the base to a corner of the cork sheet.

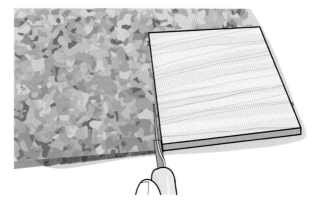

2   Press down on the plywood with one hand to keep it in position on the cork. Use the craft knife to cut the cork. This doesn't need to be perfect; the cork will be trimmed again once the glue is dry.

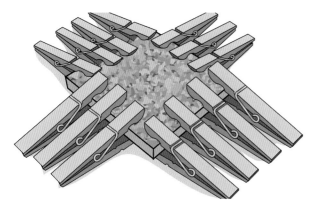

3   Clamp the base and the cork firmly together with clothespins. When the glue is thoroughly dry, trim the cork again and sand the edges smooth. Wipe the cork to remove any dust before starting step 4.

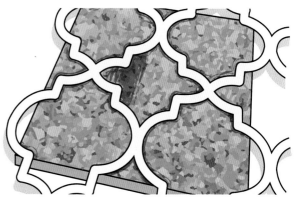

4   Prepare your stencil (pages 116–117) and use the permanent marker or acrylic paint and paintbrush to apply the design to the upper surface of the coaster. When dry, apply a coat of sealer.

Plant labels

If you need a simple, quick, durable, and cunningly resourceful way to organize your urban garden, try this project. All you need is wine corks, a permanent waterproof marker, skewers, and five minutes! With colored markers, you could even color-code the tops of the corks so that plants can be easily spotted.

You will need

- 1 wine cork for each label
- Permanent waterproof marker
- 1 bamboo skewer for each label
- Scissors or pliers

How to make the plant labels

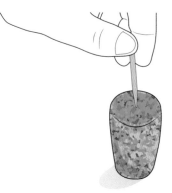

1 Write plant name on the neck of the cork using the marker. Add planting date or color-coding now as well.

2 Push the pointed end of the skewer into the bottom of the cork. Don't push too hard or the cork may split.

3 Trim the skewer if necessary using scissors or pliers. Plant your label alongside the plant. How easy and effective is that?!

Finishing touch

For more garden fun, use exterior household paint to undercoat the corks in white, and when dry apply a second coat in a different color. Instead of skewers, repurpose old forks.

Earrings

This is one of my most favorite upcycled wine cork projects! Be warned—it is addictive, especially when people always compliment you on your gorgeous jewelry. Old stationery, tear sheets from magazines, handmade and origami papers, fabric, or freehand drawing or painting can be used to create the finished look. Follow the core steps to make decorative buttons or a pendant and brooch instead. This is the perfect project for an assembly line setup so you can make lots of earrings in one fun session!

You will need

- Cutting mat
- Wine cork (1 cork will make 3 pairs of earrings)
- Craft knife, bread knife, handsaw, or hacksaw
- Scissors
- White glue and paintbrush
- 2 small screw-in eyelets
- 2 jewelry jump rings
- 2 earring hooks
- Wood varnish to create a resin-type finish (optional)
- Decorative paper

How to make the earrings

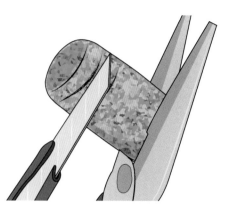

1 Hold the cork with a pair of pliers. On the cutting mat, cut two ¼ inch (6 mm) disks from the cork using a craft knife. Trim and neaten the edges with the scissors.

2 Apply white glue with a paintbrush to one side of each disk. Press the glued sides to the back of your chosen paper or fabric. Allow to dry.

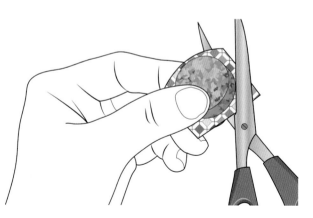

3 Use scissors to trim excess paper from around each disk carefully and precisely. Place the disks paper-side up and apply a coat of white glue to the upper surfaces. Leave to dry.

4 Screw an eyelet into the edge of each disk. Thread a jump ring through each eyelet, and then thread an earring hook to the jump ring. Close the jump ring. Your earrings are now ready to wear!

Toy boat

Upcycling wine corks into a toy boat is a fun project for young and old! The boat is easy to make and there is minimal mess and fuss. Start with the basic boat model, and then get really creative with materials and decoration for the sails, cork hull, and deck. This boat floats reliably and is so sweet, you will have a fleet in no time. Perhaps you had better make plans for a cork dock as well?

You will need

- 3 wine corks for each toy boat
- Wood glue
- Cutting mat
- 4 colored rubberbands per boat
- Bamboo skewer
- Pliers or scissors
- Construction paper, repurposed greeting card, or patterned wrapping paper (strengthen this by gluing it to cardboard first)
- Craft knife
- One-hole punch (optional)
- Screw-in eyelet
- Hemp cord

How to make the toy boat

1 Glue the three corks side by side to make the boat's hull and deck. Wrap rubberbands around the corks while the glue dries. Do not discard the bands—keep them in place around the corks and even add some more to make racing stripes!

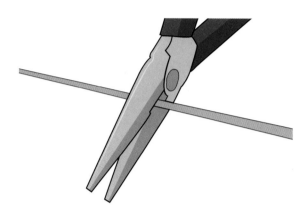

2 Use the pliers or scissors to trim the skewer to 4–5 inches (10–12.5 cm) in length for the mast.

3 Draw the outline of a triangular sail (about 2½ x 3 inches/6.5 x 12.5 cm) onto paper or card. On the cutting mat, use the craft knife to cut out the sail and to cut two very small slits across the sail about ¾ inch (2 cm) from the shortest side and ¾ inch (2 cm) from the opposite corner. If using stiffened paper, make holes using the one-hole punch. Thread the skewer, pointed end down, through the slits.

4 Cut out a small flag and attach it to the top of the mast. Push the point end of the skewer into the center of the middle cork. Screw an eyelet into the "bow" of the boat and attach a length of hemp cord so that the boat can be pulled along. It's time to go boating!

Fridge magnet

Making a fridge magnet is never boring! It's fun for all ages and cost effective because you are repurposing discarded items. Once you have made a simple cork fridge magnet, it's easy to add some pizzazz with funky paper, old jewelry, and buttons. The more practical among you can hand-letter the magnets with messages like "To do," "To get," and "To pay" that will help impose order on the chaos of a busy life. You will find magnets in many sizes and shapes in craft stores.

> CRAFT MIX AND MATCH
Stenciling (page 116)
Stamping (page 118)
Painting (page 128)

You will need

- Wine cork (enough to make 5–6 fridge magnets)
- Magnet, ¼–½-inch (0.5–1.5 cm) diameter
- Craft knife, bread knife, hand saw, or hacksaw
- Cutting mat
- Scissors
- Craft glue and paintbrush or glue gun and glue sticks
- Paper, fabric, beads, buttons, glitter, felt-tip pens, and other items to decorate the magnet

How to make the fridge magnet

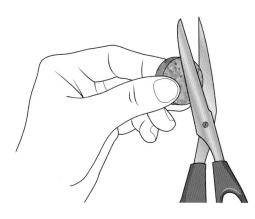

1 Cut a disk ¼-inch (6-mm) thick from the wine cork using the knife or saw. Cut slowly to avoid tearing the cork. Neaten the edges with the scissors.

2 Glue the magnet to the back of the disk. Leave to dry.

3 Decorate the front of the fridge magnet with glued and trimmed paper or fabric; buttons, beads, or glitter; hand-lettered words or names; or a stenciled, stamped, or painted design.

TIP

If you want to carve a shape or a letter into the cork in the style of a stamp (page 118), cut the cork disk ½ inch (1.5 cm) thick and follow the same steps as on page 68 for making the stamp.

Place card holder

If you are planning a dinner party or a wedding reception, here is the DIY project for you! Wine cork place card holders are a simple and cost effective way to indicate where your guests are seated. Take your time cutting and trimming; your hard work could be ruined with one wrong cut. For the name cards, upcycle old greeting cards or cereal boxes, and stencil or stamp your designs onto the place cards, then write the guests' names.

› CRAFT MIX AND MATCH
  Stenciling (page 116)
  Stamping (page 118)

You will need

- Wine cork (1 cork per place card holder)
- Craft knife, bread knife, hand saw, or hacksaw
- Cutting mat
- Scissors
- Sandpaper and a flat block of wood

How to make the place card holder

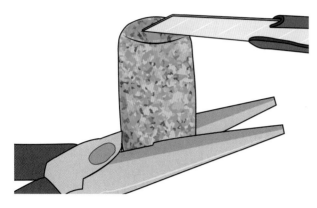

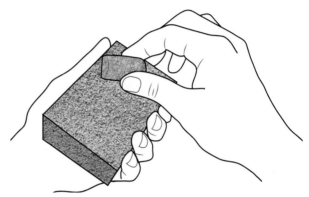

1 On the cutting mat use the knife or saw to cut off a ¼-inch (6-mm) slice along the length of the cork. This will give the cork a flat base on which to sit. Trim any rough edges with the scissors.

2 Wrap a strip of sandpaper around the wood block. Sandpaper the cut side so that it's smooth and even. This will ensure the bottom is universally flat.

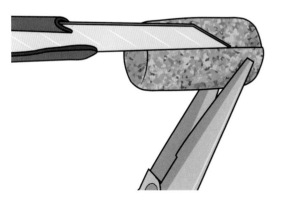

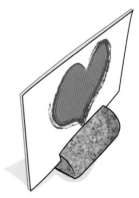

3 Use the craft knife to cut a vertical slit, about half the depth of the cork, along the length of the rounded side of the cork. Make sure the slit is straight and runs along the center of the cork.

4 Make a second cut along the cork, parallel and very close to the first and at a slight angle. The second cut will intersect with the first. Remove the loose cork from between the two cuts. This groove will make it easier to slot the place card into the holder.

Chunky ring

If you are looking for one-of-a-kind jewelry for yourself or for friends, look no further. Upcycled wine corks make swanky jewelry, including rings. For minimal cash outlay and time, you can create unique rings that everyone will love. Once the basic chunky ring is made, you can look at ways to decorate it. Among the many decorating ideas, the easiest is to glue paper, fabric, beads, or buttons to the top. Craft stores or jewelry findings suppliers will have many different styles of ring settings from which you can choose.

You will need

- Wine cork (enough to make 4–5 rings)
- Craft knife, bread knife, hand saw, or hacksaw
- Cutting mat
- Scissors
- Sandpaper wrapped around a block of wood
- Cyanoacrylate glue or contact cement
- Metal ring setting with a flat mount
- Clothespin
- Decorating items like beads, buttons, paper, and fabric

How to make the chunky ring

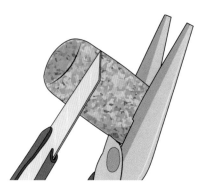

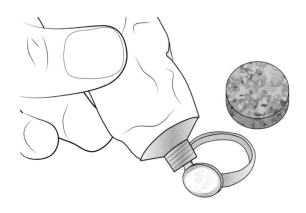

1 Cut a disk ¼-inch (6-mm) thick from the cork using the knife or saw. Cut slowly and carefully to prevent tearing the cork. Trim the edges of the disk with the scissors. Make sure the faces and edge of the disk are smooth and even. This can be done by rubbing the disk on sandpaper wrapped around a wood block.

2 Apply a couple of drops of glue or contact cement onto the flat mount on the ring setting.

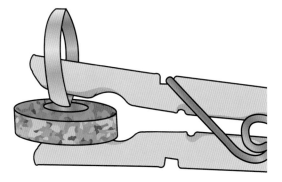

3 Clamp the cork disk and ring between the jaws of a clothespin. Leave to dry.

4 That is all you need to do to make the basic chunky ring. Now, have some fun with the decorating. You can use some of the techniques for creating the magnet (page 82), or choose some from chapter five.

Mixed Materials

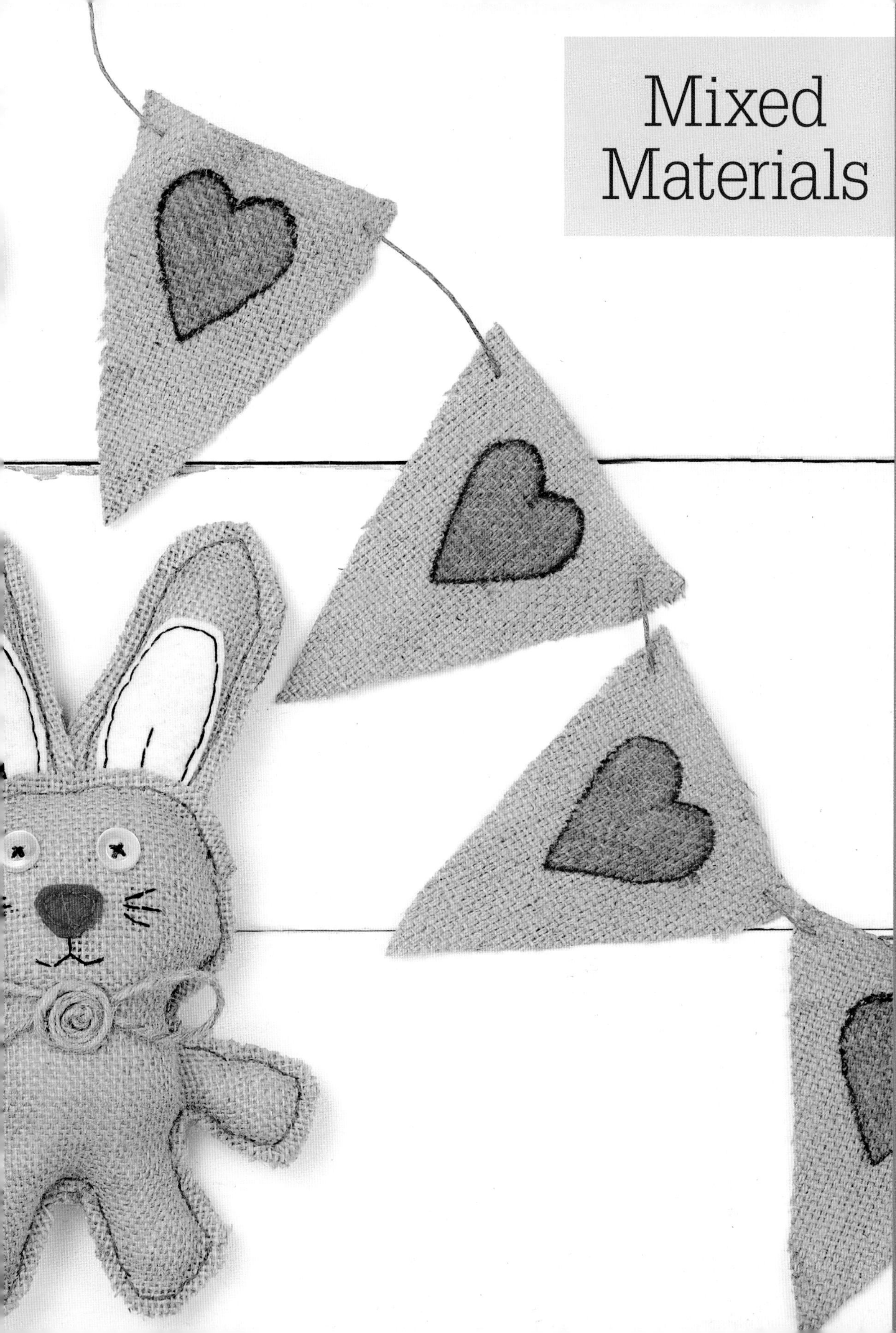

Overview

To add more interest, texture, and creativity to your projects, use a combination of two or more materials. Sometimes it's enough to use materials from the same family, like jute with burlap, or you can be innovative and mix and match across a range of materials. You are only limited by your imagination and the treasures you find in your craft box, recycling bin, and from places wider afield.

Popular mixed materials projects are the burlap and jute photo frame and gift bag; the cork and burlap keepsake display; and the jute and burlap bird ornament and toy rabbit. You will not believe how a small scrap of felt or upholstery or sewing fabric, some beads, and repurposed jewelry can elevate the finished item, while minimizing costs and maximizing creativity.

With crafting and especially upcycling there are no hard and fast rules to what you use and how to execute your projects. When following the projects in this chapter, the materials list is a guide only; adjust it to suit the materials you have and that you want to use. Like any recipe you can always switch supplies and skip or modify some steps. For example, work through one of the projects and add your own innovations and materials. Every time I look at a project I can always see ways of making it better or different or more to my taste, but the two ingredients that cannot be forgotten are imagination and fun!

Pinboard

A pinboard is a useful item in your home or office, and it's a fun way to restyle an old picture frame. Why not repurpose a thrift store corkboard for this DIY? What you save on cork sheets, you can spend on the burlap and the decorative finish! If using the thinner cork (as specified in the materials list below), you might want to glue the cork onto thick cardboard first. This is an easy project that does not require a huge investment in time, money, or effort.

You will need

- Picture frame
- Metal rule and pencil
- Sheet or roll of cork $^1/_8$–$^1/_4$-inch (3–6-mm) thick and the same size as the frame
- Craft knife
- Cutting mat
- Glue gun and glue sticks or white glue and spongebrush
- Burlap, no smaller than the size of the picture frame
- Clothespins
- Scissors

How to make a pinboard

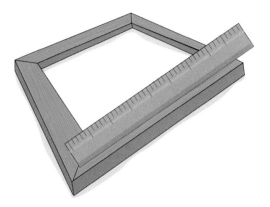

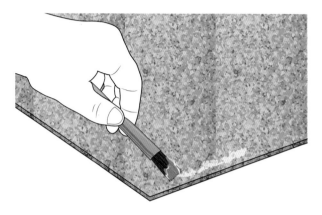

1 Measure the inset of the picture frame. Transfer these measurements to the sheet or roll of cork. Use the craft knife to cut the cork, running the craft knife along the metal rule to get straight edges. Depending on the thickness of your cork this may be a quick job or may take a bit of time. Go slowly to avoid tearing the cork.

2 Apply the glue with the spongebrush around the edges of the cork, on one side only.

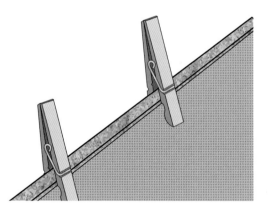

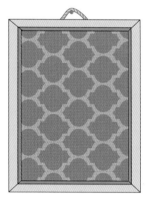

3 Lay the burlap evenly onto the cork, smoothing and pressing it over the glue. The burlap should be taut and flat. Clamp the cork and burlap with clothespins.

4 When dry, trim excess burlap from around the cork. Stenciling, stamping, and painting are good decorating options for the burlap-covered board. When embellishment is complete and dry, fix the pinboard inside the frame and attach a string so that you can hang your upcycled pinboard.

Lunch bag

A small burlap bag can be used to carry a packed lunch, a picnic-for-one, or edible treats for children. This bag, which has a drawstring close, can be edged or fully lined in a contrasting fabric, and decorated with stencils or stamps, beads and buttons, or felt appliqué and embroidery. It may be easier to do stencils, stamps, appliqué, and embroidery before the side seams are sewn. This bag will hold a generous lunch of sandwiches, fruit, something sweet, and a juice bottle, but adjust the measurements to suit your needs.

> CRAFT MIX AND MATCH
> Stenciling (page 116)
> Cross-stitch (page 122)
> Dyeing burlap (page 124)
> Felt appliqué (page 134)

You will need

- Burlap, 9 x 22 inches (23 x 55 cm)
- Ruler and chalk
- Dressmaking pins
- Iron and ironing board
- 2 lengths of jute 15 inches (38 cm) long
- 2 pieces of fabric, 2½ x 9½ inches (6.5 x 24 cm)
- 2 or more beads

How make the lunch bag

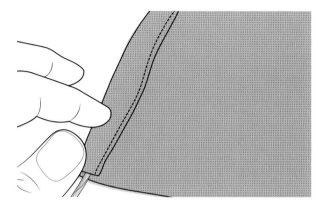

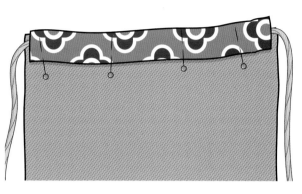

1 Fold both short sides of the burlap over ¼ inch (6 mm) and pin. Iron the folds. Remove the pins, fold again 1 inch (2.5 cm), and pin. Iron the folds and remove the pins. Insert a piece of jute under each hem. Pin, then sew along the fold, taking care not to sew over the jute.

2 Fold to wrong side and iron a ¼ inch (6 mm) hem on all edges on the two pieces of fabric. Pin one long side of each piece, right side out, 1 inch (2.5 cm) from the folded burlap hem. Fold the fabric over the burlap and pin. Sew the fabric to the burlap, taking care not to sew over the jute.

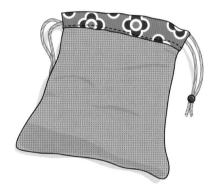

3 Fold the burlap in half across its length with hems facing out. Pin raw edges together and sew, starting from the folded end and sewing to the hemmed end, with a ½ inch (1.5 cm) seam. Stop sewing when you reach the fabric trim. Knot and cut the sewing threads.

4 Turn the bag inside out. Thread the ends of the jute on one side of the bag through one or more beads, and knot the ends together to secure the bead. Repeat for the jute ends on the other side of the bag.

Photo frame

Mix it up by using burlap and jute to customize a new photo frame or to rescue an old one. For this DIY you can either go a little bit country or a little bit rock 'n' roll depending on your style and décor. You may be able to source a burlap sack from your local coffee roaster; otherwise everything you need will be found in a craft store. Don't forget to wash, dry, and iron your old burlap sack if that is what you are using! I can't provide quantities for the materials used in this project as they will depend on the size of your photo frame.

You will need

- Ruler
- Photo frame
- Thick cardboard $1/8$–$1/4$ inch (3–6 mm) thick
- Craft knife and scissors
- Cutting mat
- White glue and spongebrush
- Burlap
- Stencil
- Masking tape
- Acrylic paints and paintbrush
- Photo
- 4 photo frame corners
- Clothespins
- Jute, about 1 yard (1 m) in length

TIP

Use thick cardboard for the frame inset. Thin cardboard may warp when covered with glue and burlap.

How to make the photo frame

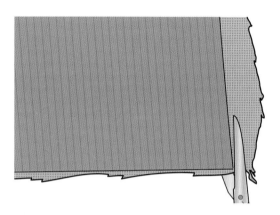

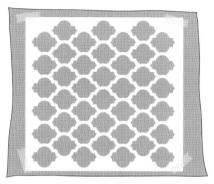

1 Measure the inset of the frame. Transfer these measurements to the cardboard. Cut it out on a cutting mat with the craft knife. Lay the burlap out on a flat work surface. Apply a coat of white glue to the cardboard, and then lay it glue-side down onto the burlap. Flip the cardboard and burlap over and smooth and press the burlap to the cardboard. Clamp with clothespins. When the glue is dry, trim excess burlap from around the cardboard.

2 Place the stencil onto the burlap and secure it in place with the tape. Fill the pattern with acrylic paint by dabbing into the cut-out sections with the brush. Allow to dry.

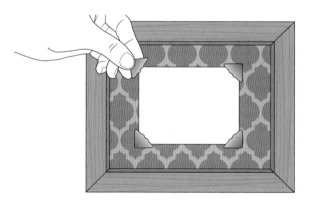

3 Position the photo on the burlap and slide the photo corners onto the photo. Glue the photo corners to the burlap. Some photo corners have an adhesive backing, but I always apply glue as well.

4 Tie a knot in a free end of the jute. Coil the jute around the knot to create a circular disk. When the circle reaches the diameter that best suits your frame, cut the jute. Adhere the jute coil to the frame with glue. Make as many jute coils as you want.

Bunting

Hemp and burlap bunting is all the rage! It's the perfect decorating solution for any celebration or to make everyday a party day. Basic bunting requires only hemp, burlap, and glue, but you can go to town on decorating it with stitching, felt, ribbon, stamps, paints, or stencils. Once you have made one string of bunting, there will be no stopping you.

> CRAFT MIX AND MATCH
  Stenciling (page 116)
  Stamping (page 118)
  Decorative edge stitch (page 120)
  Painting (page 128)
  Felt appliqué (page 134)

You will need

- Cardboard, about 7 inches (18.5 cm) square
- Pencil and ruler
- Craft knife or scissors
- Cutting mat
- Burlap, 1 square yard (1 sq m) will make about 28 7-inch (18-cm) triangles
- White glue and paintbrush
- Clothespins
- Fancy cookie cutter
- Permanent markers in a few colors
- Roll of hemp

How to make the bunting

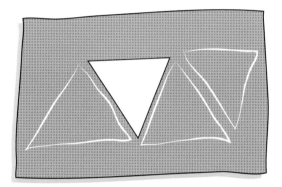

1 To make the template for the triangles: draw a square 7 x 7 inches (18 x 18 cm) onto the card. Mark the center on one side of the square. Join this point to the two corners opposite. Cut out the triangle. Spread out the burlap and trace around the template until you have enough for your bunting. Cut out the triangles.

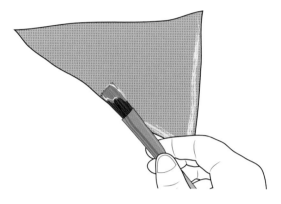

2 Brush the edges of the triangles on one side with white glue. Leave to dry.

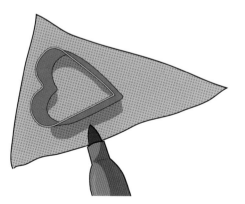

3 Lay the cookie cutter in the middle of a burlap triangle, trace around with a marker, and then fill in with a marker of a different color. Repeat to decorate all of the triangles. You can decorate just one side of the triangles or both sides.

4 Make two small holes at least ½ inch (1.5 cm) in from the top and sides of each triangle, and then weave the hemp in and out, leaving a few inches between each triangle. Allow plenty of hemp at each end of the bunting. When you are happy with the spacing and length of the bunting, dab the holes and hemp with glue to keep the triangles in place.

Keepsake display

What can you do with all those earrings and necklaces, trinkets and treasures, and souvenir tickets and photo memories? Display them, of course. Use an old picture frame, crossed with lengths of hemp or jute to create a unique mini-gallery where you can hang and peg your favorite things. I have used a vintage burlap produce bag, its screen-printed label adding a further nostalgic element to the finished look.

You will need

- Picture frame
- Metal ruler and pencil
- Sheet of cork, ½ inch (1.5 cm) thick and the same size as the frame
- Craft knife
- Cutting mat
- Glue gun and glue sticks or white glue and spongebrush
- Burlap, no smaller than the size of the picture frame
- Clothespins
- Scissors
- Screw-in eyelets, about $^5/_{16}$ inch (8 mm) in overall length, and you will need two per line of hemp or jute
- Hemp or jute

How to make the keepsake display

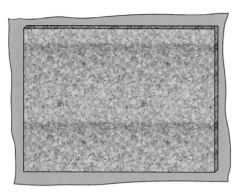

1 Follow steps 1–3 for the Pinboard (page 92). When the glue is dry, trim the excess burlap from around the cork. Turn the board over so the burlap side is face down and the top farthest from you.

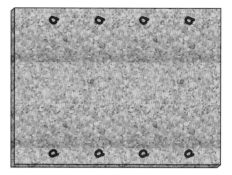

2 Depending on what you want to display and the size of your board, decide how many lines of cord you want. Measure and mark on both side edges, about 1 inch (2.5 cm) in from the edges, where each cord will start and end, making sure they are level. Dip the thread on the eyelets into white glue, and then screw the eyelets into the marked positions on the cork.

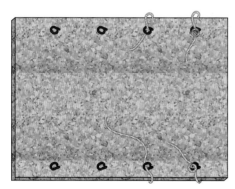

3 If you are decorating the burlap, do it now before the strings are attached. Tie the free end of the cord to the first eyelet. Bring the cord across the front of the board and then to the back of the board where it is tied and knotted to the corresponding eyelet. The cord should be taut. Cut the cord. Repeat for all remaining pairs of eyelets.

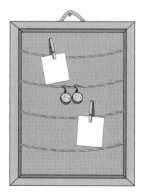

4 Insert the keepsake display into the frame. You can secure it with duct tape if the fit is not snug enough. Hang your treasures from the lengths of hemp, using paperclips and tiny pegs where necessary. If the cords sag when suspended with treasures, support the cords with decorative pushpins and thumbtacks.

Toy rabbit

This burlap and jute toy rabbit is the perfect gift for a friend or young child. If making for a child, take extra care when adding buttons and yarn or cord details, as these must be securely attached. Once you master this pattern, extend yourself and make other animal toys. The simpler the pattern, the easier it will be to sew and stuff. Wash the burlap in cold water on a gentle cycle, hang to dry, and iron before starting this project.

> CRAFT MIX AND MATCH
> Cross-stitch (page 122)
> Felt appliqué (page 134)

You will need

- Paper and pencil
- Scissors
- Chalk
- Burlap, 20 x 30 inches (51 x 76 cm) will make a rabbit that is about 8 inches (20.5 cm) from paw to paw and 13 inches (33 cm) tall
- Fabric glue and paintbrush or spongebrush
- Scrap fabric, felt, buttons, thick thread or knitting yarn, and jute
- Dressmaking pins
- Sewing machine or sewing needle and thread (embroidery floss is recommended)
- Polyester fiberfill or scrap burlap

How to make the toy rabbit

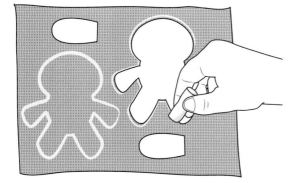

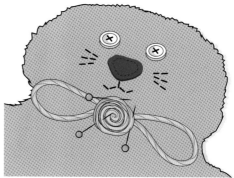

1 Draw the outline of a rabbit onto the paper. When you are happy with it, cut it out. Cut off the ears. Trace the body and ears onto the burlap. Mark these pieces "front." Flip the body and ears over and trace onto the burlap. Mark these pieces "back." Cut out the pieces and brush the edges on one side with the glue to prevent fraying. Leave to dry.

2 Stitch features to the front of the rabbit. I have used buttons for the eyes, scrap fabric for the nose, yarn for the mouth and whiskers, and jute for the bow tie. Form a figure of eight with a length of jute to make wings on the bow tie. Stitch the wings to the rabbit's neck. With another piece of jute, coil it to make the middle of the bow tie. Stitch this in place.

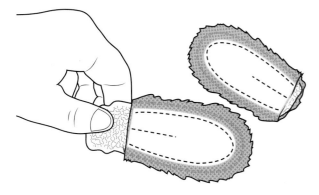

3 Cut two pieces of felt to make the insides of the rabbit's ears. Stitch these to the ears for the front of the rabbit. Pin these to the corresponding back pieces. Sew together, leaving the bottom edges open. Insert the fiberfill.

4 Pin the front and back body together and pin the ears in position, inserting the open ends between the front and back pieces. As you sew the pieces together, insert the fiberfill into the body and limbs. When most of the rabbit is sewn, add as much fiberfill as you feel is appropriate, then finish sewing.

Wine bag

Instead of using a paper gift bag when gifting wine, make a bag by upcycling burlap and jute. Create the basic wine bag and then decorate it. This is the perfect make for stenciling a design or words onto the bag, but do this before the bag is pinned and sewn. Adjust the measurements of this project to make other sizes of gift bags for preserves, oils, and homemade lotions.

> CRAFT MIX AND MATCH
Stenciling (page 116)
Stamping (page 118)
Decorative edge stitch (page 120)

You will need

- Burlap, about ¼ yard (0.25 m) is sufficient for one wine bag
- Chalk and ruler
- Scissors
- Fabric glue and paintbrush or spongebrush
- Dressmaking pins
- Iron and ironing board
- Sewing machine or sewing needle and thread
- Pencil
- Jute, 24 inches (61 cm) long
- 2 or more beads
- Hemp, jute, or embroidery floss, about 3 yards (3 m) and an embroidery needle

How to make the wine bag

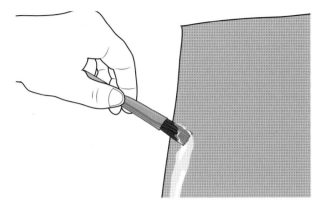

1 Depending on the size of the wine bottle, mark on the burlap with chalk a rectangle measuring 6 x 30 inches (15 x 76 cm). Cut out the rectangle and apply glue to the edges on one side of the burlap to prevent fraying. Leave to dry.

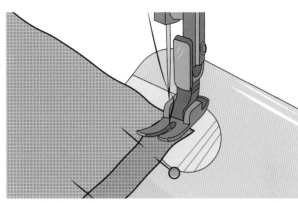

2 Fold, to the wrong side, a double ½ inch (1.5 cm) hem on the short edges, pin and iron, and then sew. Fold the burlap in half across its length. Pin the long sides together. The fold forms the bottom of the bag. Sew the long sides, leaving a ¼-inch (6-mm) seam along each long side. I started at the fold, sewed to the opening, and then reversed the bag and sewed back to the fold.

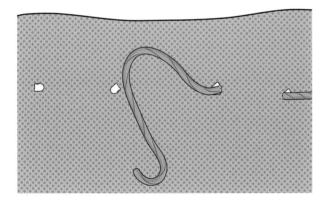

3 Turn the bag right side out. Draw a line 4 inches (10 cm) from the top of the opening on both sides of the bag. Use the pencil to make four holes along each line. Manually thread the jute in and out of the holes so that the loose ends meet at the front of the bag. Thread on the beads and tie knots to secure the beads.

4 Blanket-stitch (pages 120–121) the edges around the opening using the hemp, jute, or embroidery floss. Insert the bottle into the bag and pull on the jute ties to gather it around the neck of the bottle. Tie the jute into a bow. What a lovely way to give a bottle of wine to a host!

Lavender sachet

A lavender-filled burlap sachet is an easy DIY and it makes the perfect memorable gift. You can keep the sachet natural, with little or no embellishment, or really push the decorative boat out. The sachet can be square or shaped. Use large, fancy cookie cutters as templates for heart-, flower-, or star-shaped sachets. You can purchase loose lavender in a tea store, and one pound (0.4 kg) is enough to make about 12 sachets.

> CRAFT MIX AND MATCH
   Stenciling (page 116)
   Cross-stitch (page 122)
   Bleaching burlap (page 126)
   Felt appliqué (page 134)

You will need

- 2 pieces of burlap 4 inches (10 cm) square
- Ruler and chalk
- White glue and paintbrush
- Dressmaking pins
- Sewing needle and thread or a sewing machine
- Loose lavender
- Tablespoon
- Funnel (or make one with a cone of paper)
- 1 piece of hemp 6 inches (15 cm) in length
- Scissors

How to make the lavender sachet

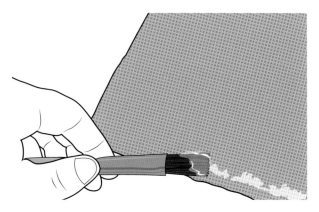

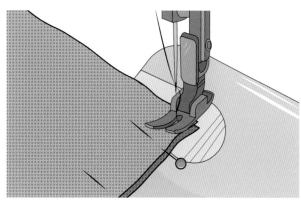

1 Apply white glue to the edges of both squares to prevent fraying. Leave to dry. If you are decorating the sachet, do it now before you start sewing.

2 Place one square on top of the other and pin together around the sides. Hand- or machine-sew three sides, leaving a ¼ inch (6 mm) seam.

3 Spoon 3–5 tablespoons of lavender into the sachet. The funnel will make this job easy. Pin the open side of the sachet, then hand- or machine-sew, leaving a ¼-inch (6-mm) seam.

4 Make a small hole halfway along one side or in a corner, and thread through the hemp. Knot the loose ends together to make a hanging loop for the sachet. Trim ends if required.

Napkin ring

Burlap and cork are a great combination, and napkin rings are a simple way to jazz up your table setting. It is easy enough to create a funky napkin ring, but do not stop there. You can also modify the steps to make festive seasonal party crackers that could be filled with a small gift, surprise, and silly riddle!

> ❯ CRAFT MIX AND MATCH
> Stamping (page 118)
> Felt appliqué (page 134)

You will need

- Cardboard tube from center of a toilet roll (makes 2 napkin rings)
- Scissors
- Burlap, about 3 x 6 inches (7.5 x 15 cm) for each napkin ring
- Fabric or craft glue and paintbrush or spongebrush
- Clothespins
- 2 lengths of lace or ribbon, about 6 inches (15 cm) long
- Glue gun and glue sticks (optional)
- ¼-inch (6-mm) thick disk cut from a wine cork
- Craft knife
- Metal or fiber washer the same diameter or smaller than the cork disk

How to make the napkin ring

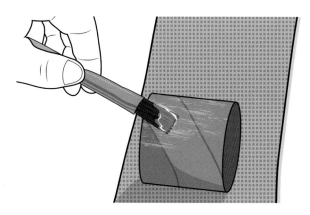

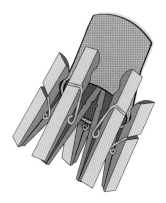

1 Cut the cardboard tube in half across its length. Apply glue to the outside of the tube. Lay the tube onto the middle of the burlap, with the open ends of the tube facing the long sides of the burlap.

2 Wrap the burlap around the tube, overlapping the two short ends. Apply glue to the inside of the tube and fold and press the edges inside the tube. Hold the burlap in place with clothespins while the glue dries.

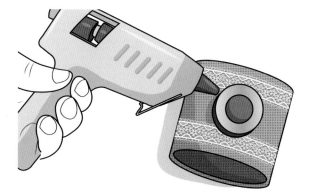

Party cracker

Cut burlap to 6 x 12 inches (15 x 30 cm). Apply glue to the edges of the burlap and allow to dry. When completely dry, apply glue to an uncut cardboard tube and wrap the burlap around it. When finished, insert treats into the tube, and tie the ends with jute. Decorate the cracker to suit the occasion.

3 Glue the piece of lace or ribbon around the tube. Clamp with clothespins while the glue dries. Glue the cork disk to the napkin ring. Glue the washer to the cork disk.

Bird ornament

You can create a super cute, seasonal or year-round ornament out of burlap and jute in a jiffy. You can design your own pattern or use a bird-shaped cookie cutter for the template. The ornament is filled to give it shape, and buttons, odd bits of jewelry, felt, and hemp can be used for details like eyes and wings. This is another of those projects where you can set up an assembly line and make a flock of birds in one session.

> CRAFT MIX AND MATCH
  Cross-stitch (page 122)
  Felt appliqué (page 134)

You will need

- Scrap cardboard and pencil, or a cookie cutter
- Scissors
- Burlap (the amount will depend on the size of your ornament)
- Chalk
- White glue and paintbrush
- 2 buttons
- Jute
- Dressmaking pins
- Embroidery thread (split six threads down to three threads) and needle (optional)
- Polyester fiberfill or scrap burlap

How to make the bird ornament

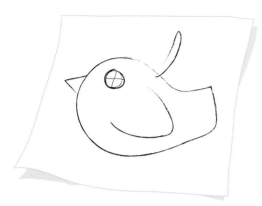

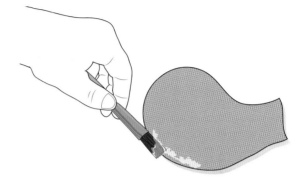

1 Draw the outline of your bird onto cardboard. Draw the beak separately. Aim for the bird to measure no more than 5 inches (12.5 cm) in length or height. Cut out the bird's body and beak to make the templates.

2 Trace the templates (or trace around the cookie cutter) in chalk onto the burlap. Flip the templates or cutter over, place them on the burlap, and trace around them. You now have front and back pieces for the body and beak. Cut out the pieces and brush the edges on one side with glue. Leave to dry.

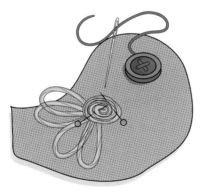

3 As both sides of the ornament will be seen, decorate the front and back of the bird. I used old buttons for the eyes, and spirals and loops of jute for the wings. You can attach the decorations with glue or with hand stitching.

4 Lay the beak pieces on top of each other. Pin the front and back together, decoration facing out, and sandwich the beak between these pieces. Hand sew the body pieces together, but leave a section unsewn to insert the fiberfill. Sew the opening closed. Hand sew the beak pieces together. Thread a piece of jute through the top of the ornament and knot the ends to make a hanging loop.

Decorations & Embellishments

Overview

In this chapter we'll explore easy and cost-effective techniques that will add "bling" to your DIYs. In some instances, the decoration is added at the start of the project, sometimes midway through, or at the end. Whatever processes the project requires, the essence is to plan ahead, and so before making that first cut, read up on the options for decorating or embellishing your DIY and gather your supplies.

With experience you will pick up tricks, but here's a few tips to get you on your way. Test dye a scrap of the burlap you are using for a project (burlap varies from batch to batch and will take up dye differently, so test on the actual project fabric) to check that the color is correct and strong enough. Bleaching burlap is a bit tricky, so get your technique down before taking the plunge. A craft failure (and I have had many!) sometimes results in a surprisingly welcome outcome; if not, then rack it up to experience. It is a good idea to stencil fabric before you create your final project, especially if it's a repeat or all-over pattern. If it's a single motif, use chalk to mark the outline of the stencil so that you position it precisely.

I recommend that you get everything you need together and check quantities before starting on a project. There's nothing worse than beginning to dye a piece of burlap and then realizing that you don't have enough dye; or getting partway through a stencil and running out of paint or finding that the felt-tip pen has dried up.

You can refer to the techniques in this chapter when working on projects beyond the ones in this book: lots of fabrics can be bleached or dyed; furniture can be stenciled; and felt appliqué can be used on leather and many other fabrics. There are no boundries where craft and creativity are concerned!

Stenciling

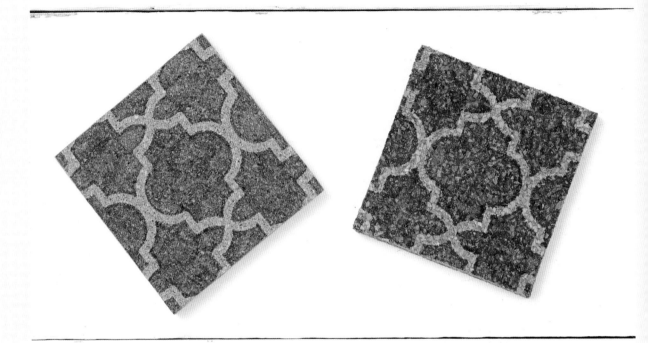

Stenciling is the perfect embellishment for burlap and cork projects. You can purchase, as I did, ready-cut stencils from craft, art, and dollar stores. There is an abundance of designs available and stencils are cost- and time-effective, or you can cut your own using a sheet of transparent plastic. The easiest way to color a stencil is with permanent felt-tip pens, but for more finicky designs and solid color-fill, use acrylic paints and a spongebrush.

You will need

- Burlap or cork surface
- Store-bought stencil
- Thick permanent felt-tip pens or acrylic paints and paintbrush
- Masking tape

TIP

If stenciling burlap, wash, dry, and iron prior to applying the stencil. Depending on the project, it's often best to stencil straight onto the fabric once the pattern has been traced or cut and prior to commencing sewing and other construction.

How to do stenciling

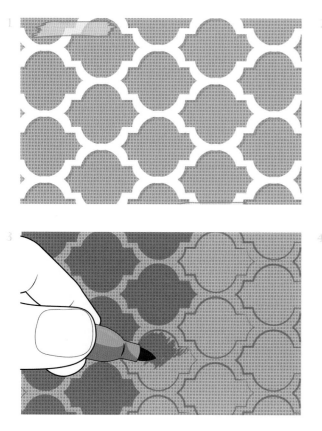

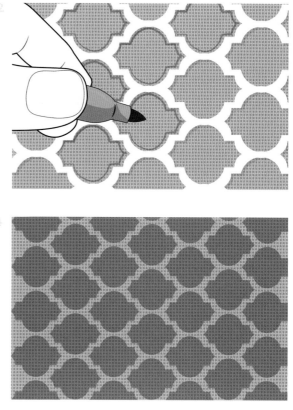

1 Wash your fabric and ensure it's dust free. Outline or cut your pattern so you know where to position the stencil. Tape the stencil securely to the burlap or cork with masking tape.

2 Trace the outline of the stencil using a felt-tip pen. If using paint: dip the tip of the paintbrush into the paint and dab the brush into the stencil. Don't overload the brush with paint, but keep dabbing until the stencil is filled and the color is dense. If there is too much paint on the brush, the paint may seep under the stencil and give a very splotchy finish.

3 When the felt-tip outline or paint is dry and you are happy with the coverage and strength of the paint color, remove the stencil. Lift the stencil straight up as there may be wet paint on the back of the stencil. If using felt-tips, fill the stencil outlines with solid color.

4 Clean up the edges of your stenciled design with a felt-tip and you're ready to finish constructing your project. Such an easy and effective way to create something unique and personal with very simple materials like burlap and cork.

Stamping

Stamping is a fun way to add a design to cork and burlap projects and, of course, to other surfaces like paper, wood, and glass. Craft and art stores stock quality ink stamp pads, stamping inks, and ready-made stamps if you don't want to make your own. Acrylic paint can be used instead of ink. Always test your stamp on a scrap of the material to be printed on using the stamping ink or paint before getting stuck into embellishing a project.

TIP

Keep the design for the stamp simple and use a sharp craft knife. It can help to clamp wine corks in a vise or pair of pliers when cutting. The vise or pliers will also keep fingers well away from the sharp blade!

You will need

- Wine cork
- Pen
- Craft knife
- Vise or pliers to hold cork while cutting (optional)
- Ink stamping pad and stamping ink or acrylic paint and shallow palette
- Cork, burlap or other fabric, wood, card, or paper on which to print the stamp

How to do stamping

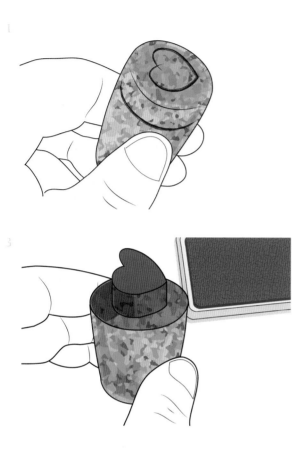

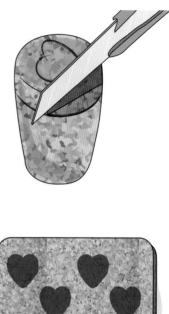

1. Draw a design onto the flat top of the wine cork, and then draw a line around the neck of the cork ¼ inch (6 mm) down from the top.

2. Cut vertically down about ¼ inch (6 mm) following the outline of your design. Now make horizontal cuts into the line around the neck of the cork to a depth where the vertical and horizontal cuts intersect. Sections of cork should fall away leaving the stamp in relief. Cut slowly to avoid tearing the cork.

3. Test the stamp on a scrap piece of the material to be decorated. Make adjustments to the stamp if required. Press the stamp onto the ink pad or into a shallow pool of acrylic paint. Check that the stamp is covered with ink or paint.

4. Press the stamp straight down and firmly onto the printing surface. Try not to let the stamp wobble left or right. Lift the stamp straight up and allow the ink or paint to dry before stamping again in close proximity. It is a good idea to occasionally wash the stamp to keep the edges sharp.

Decorative edge stitch

It is often a simple touch that turns the lovely into the pretty fabulous. One of these simple touches is embroidery. I use a blanket-stitch on so many of my craft projects. It adds an elegant touch to felt appliqué (pages 134–135) and is in keeping with burlap's stripped-back appeal. Blanket-stitch comes into its own to seam two pieces of fabric together and to finish an unhemmed edge. You can find embroidery floss in a wide range of colors, including metallic, at craft and dollar stores.

You will need

- Fabric to be joined or edged
- Dressmaking pins
- Embroidery floss and embroidery needle
- Scissors

TIP

Split the strands of the embroidery floss from six strands to three unless you specifically want bulky edging stitches, and use an embroidery needle as the eye is larger than that on a regular sewing needle.

How to do decorative edge stitch

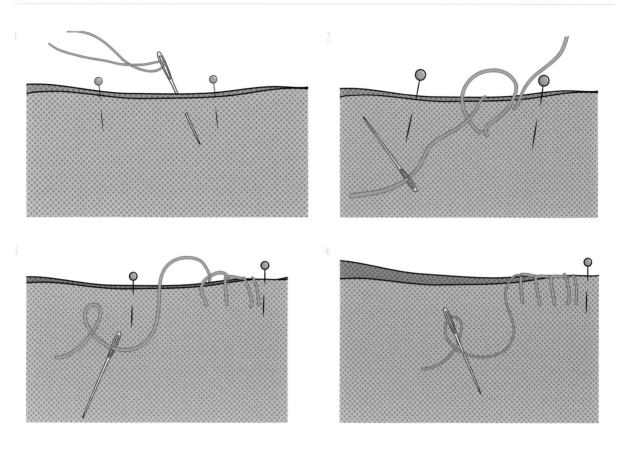

1 Prepare the fabric for stitching. Burlap, for example, should be washed in cold water on a gentle cycle, hanged to dry, and ironed. Pin the seam to be stitched. Thread the needle with the floss. Pull the needle through the top piece of fabric so the free end of the floss is sandwiched between the layers of fabric.

2 Insert the needle back through the top layer, just alongside the initial stitch, and through the bottom layer of fabric. Pull the thread to create a loop, as shown. Put the needle through the loop, pull gently to tighten the thread and to set the holding stitch.

3 Insert the needle, about ¼ inch (6 mm) to the left of the holding stitch, down through both layers, keeping the needle in front and to the right of the thread.

4 Pull to tighten the stitch. The thread will "lay" on the top edge of the fabric. Repeat steps 2–4 to finish edge stitching the seam. To tie off, pull the needle through the bottom layer and tie a knot between the two layers. Trim excess thread.

Cross-stitch

Cross-stitch is an easy way to jazz up some of the projects in this book, especially those using burlap as the core ingredient. But even something like cork sheet or thin cork disks can be cross-stitched! You can follow the weave of the burlap to give you a grid for your cross-stitch pattern. All you need is an embroidery needle and embroidery floss, but a hoop to tension the fabric is a very useful tool and helps keep stitches evenly tensioned.

You will need

- Burlap or other fabric
- Embroidery needle and embroidery floss
- Scissors
- Cross-stitch hoop (optional)

TIP

It can be awkward to cross-stitch a constructed item like a bag, so it is best to do the decorative stitching prior to pinning or sewing.

How to cross-stitch

1. Split the embroidery floss from six strands into three, and then thread the embroidery needle. Do not knot the free end of the thread, just leave 3 inches (7.5 cm) of thread trailing on the wrong side when you make the first stitch. Push the needle up through one of the holes in the weave to the right side of the fabric.

2. You can keep your stitches consistent in size by counting x-holes up or down and left or right. Here, I counted one hole to the right and one hole down, and then pushed the needle through to the wrong side of the fabric. Next, I brought the needle through to the right side, one hole to the left, then going through again to the wrong side two holes up and to the right.

3. Now you have a full first cross-stitch. Repeat step 2 to make more cross-stitches in a row or column, a staggered pattern, or to create a shape. Don't pull too hard on the thread, keep it taut; if you pull too hard the burlap will buckle and warp.

4. Add definition to your cross-stitch pattern by outlining the shape with a simple running stitch in a contrasting color.

Dyeing burlap

Be warned: dyeing fabric can become addictive! Once you find the right dye product, you'll be dyeing everything! There are many dye products available at craft and dollar stores; take time to read the packaging, the instructions, and to get recommendations from those in-the-know. There are dye products that do not require a setup tantamount to a moon landing!

You will need

- Dye product and ingredients or items stated on the packaging
- Burlap (or other fabric) to be dyed
- Rubber gloves
- Large stainless steel bowl
- Wooden spoon

TIP

If you're not sure of the color you've chosen, do a test on a swatch of the burlap first. I find it much easier to dye the burlap before getting started on the actual project.

How to dye burlap

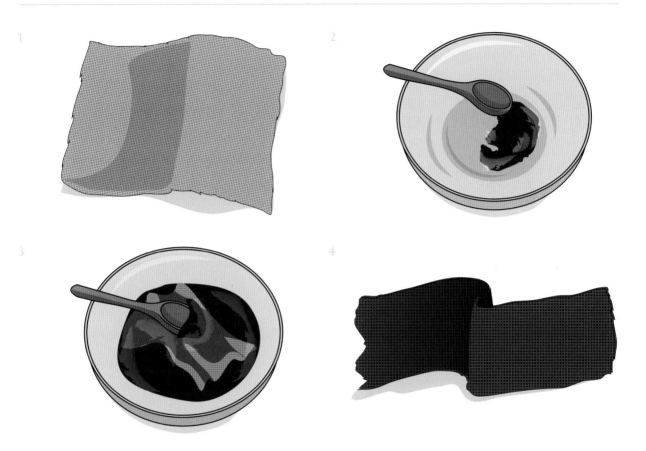

1 Wash the burlap before dyeing. If you're repurposing burlap sacks this is critical to optimize the effect of the dye. Unstitch sacks before starting to dye them.

2 Put on the rubber gloves. Prepare the ingredients following the instructions on the packaging. The dye I use requires that salt be added, and I found it best to add the salt first, followed by the dye. I then pour in the hot water and stir with a wooden spoon.

3 Soak the fabric in the dye and stir the mixture, following the instructions on the dye packaging.

4 Remove the burlap from the dye and run the burlap under cold water to remove excess dye. The next step is to wash the fabric to remove excess dye. Some fabrics, like burlap, are best washed by hand (keep the rubber gloves on) in cold water and hung to dry.

Bleaching burlap

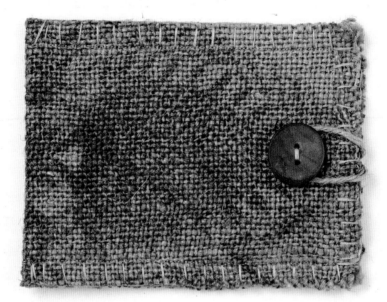

This neat little trick yields surprising results! You can create a pattern, shape, letter, or graphic on a piece of burlap with the careful application of bleach. In this project I cut out a leaf pattern on paper to create my stencil. It is best to do the bleaching before starting on the craft project. A well-ventilated room is vital for this process, as is protecting your skin, eyes, and clothing with long gloves, goggles, and a plastic cover-all apron. Make sure that children and pets are excluded while you do the bleaching, and that the work surface is protected.

You will need

- Old cloth to protect the work surface
- Burlap
- Lace or plastic doily, store-bought stencil, or make your own by cutting a pattern into a sheet of plastic
- Spray bottle
- Concentrated (undiluted) bleach
- Rubber gloves, goggles, and plastic cover-all apron

TIP

For the most effective bleach pattern, use a stencil that exposes large, rather than small, areas of the burlap to the bleach. A stencil with lots of minute detail is a poor choice for the bleaching technique.

How to bleach burlap

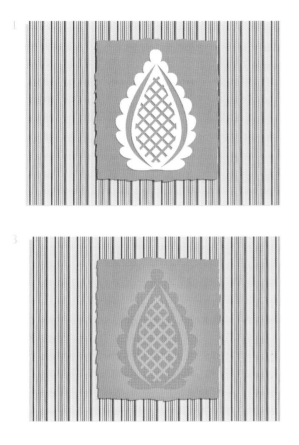

1 Spread the cloth over the work surface. Lay and smooth the burlap on top of the cloth. Place the stencil in position onto the burlap.

2 Put on your protective clothing. Pour the bleach into the spray bottle. Spray bleach thoroughly onto the doily or stencil.

3 Leave the stencil in place for 20–30 minutes to allow the bleach to work on the exposed burlap. To test if the bleach has done its job, carefully lift up one section of the stencil. Leave for a longer period or spray on more bleach if required.

4 Remove the stencil and soak the burlap in cold water before hand- or machine-washing in cold water on a gentle cycle separately. Allow to dry, and then the burlap is ready to be used in your craft project.

Painting

Cork is a particularly willing recipient of painted decoration because it is smooth, but burlap- and cord-based projects will also benefit. Choose strong, bright acrylic paint colors applied in layers with a spongebrush or paintbrush. Protect your work surface, and if using a spray sealer, apply it in a well-ventilated room or, preferably, outdoors.

TIP

Apply paint sparingly and build up layers of paint, allowing each layer to dry before applying the next layer of paint, to build up the color to the desired strength.

You will need

- Cork, burlap, or jute surface
- Pencil
- Spongebrush or paintbrush
- Acrylic paints
- Masking tape
- Scissors
- Spray sealer (optional)

How to do painting

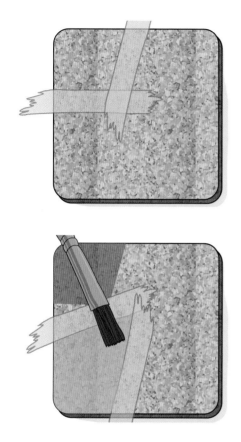

1 Make sure the surface to be painted, in this case cork, is clean, grease-free, and dust-free. Trace or draw your pattern or shape onto the cork in pencil, or mark the first element of the design (as shown in step 1) using pieces of masking tape. Press the tape firmly onto the cork and smooth any ripples or creases.

2 Apply a layer of paint to the area inside the masking tape. Allow to dry.

3 Apply further layers of paint to get the color you want. When you are satisfied and the paint is dry, remove the masking tape. Mask off a further section of your design, and repeat steps 1–3.

4 When you have completed your design and the paint is dry, apply a coat of spray sealer (optional) to protect the painting.

Knotting and beading

A great way to add bling to braided cords is to incorporate beads.
Jute and hemp projects are perfect for adding one-of-a-kind
beads (craft and bead stores stock a breathtaking array) or to
repurpose beads from unwanted, broken, or pre-loved jewelry.
I love repurposing thrift store jewelry finds into my projects!
Whatever beads you choose, they must have a large center hole,
otherwise they will not thread onto the cord or cords. In this
technique, I will show you two useful knotting techniques that
make it easy to integrate beads.

You will need

- 2 pieces of hemp or jute
  48 inches (122 cm) in
  length, in one or two
  colors
- Beads
- Work surface (see Tip)
- Scissors

TIP
Knotting and beading is easier if the cords are attached to a hook or
nail that is fixed to a smooth surface, or are gripped by the clamp
on a clipboard. Even better, angle your work surface upward a little.
Make sure you are working under a good source of light!

How to do knotting and beading

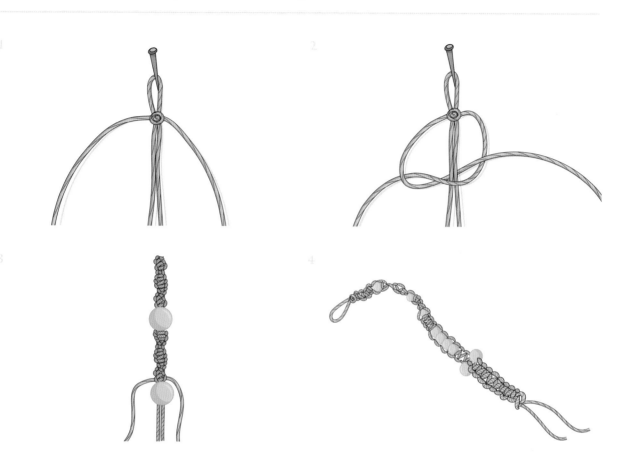

1. Secure the midpoint of one cord, and knot the midpoint of the other cord around the first cord, about ½ inch (1.5 cm) below the top of the loop. Thread the right blue cord under the red cords and over the left blue cord. Thread the left blue cord over the red cords, through the loop on the right and under the blue cord.

2. Pull on the cords to set the knot. Repeat, but thread the cord that is now on the right over the red cords, and the cord that is now on left under the red cords. These two knots make one square knot. Make square knots for 1 inch (2.5 cm).

3. Thread a bead onto each blue cord. To make a spiral knot: follow the steps for the square knot, but the right blue cord is **always** threaded under the red cords, and the left blue cord is **always** threaded over the red cords. Thread beads onto cords to create a pattern you like. Make spiral knots for 2 inches (5 cm).

4. Keep knotting until there are only 2–3 inches (5–7.5 cm) of loose cord, then knot all four cords together. Trim uneven cord ends.

Iron-on transfers

Another fun way to add decoration to your DIYs is using transfer paper. You can find a variety of options at your local craft store, but always consider the surface texture and color of your base material. Iron-on transfers can be a little pricey and finicky to work with successfully, but they add a lot to a finished craft project. Read the instructions carefully and have a good iron to hand.

TIP

A good iron that has a clean, scorch-free plate will help guarantee a successful transfer. Follow the instructions for the transfer paper carefully as some brands require specialized treatment and processing.

You will need

- A clean burlap or cork surface
- Paper and pen, creative software package, or downloaded online designs
- Scanner (optional) and printer
- Transfer paper
- Iron and ironing board
- Scissors

How to do iron-on transfers

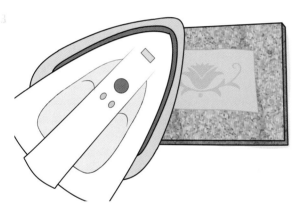

1. Create your design on paper or use a creative software package like Adobe or Microsoft. You can also find free designs online that you can download. Scan your design if required, and then print the design onto the transfer paper.

2. If the transfer is being applied to fabric, iron the fabric smooth. For other surfaces, like cork, just make sure the surface is clean and grease-free. Trim the transfer paper around the design (sometimes it's best to trim close as some transfers leave behind a film that may spoil the final look). Place the transfer right side down on the surface to be printed.

3. Set the iron to the temperature stated on the transfer paper instructions. Check that the steam is off! Press the iron evenly onto the transfer for the time recommended. Make sure the whole design is heated. Remove iron and allow the transfer to cool.

4. Peel the transfer paper away slowly and carefully. The design should now be transferred onto the surface of your craft project.

Felt appliqué

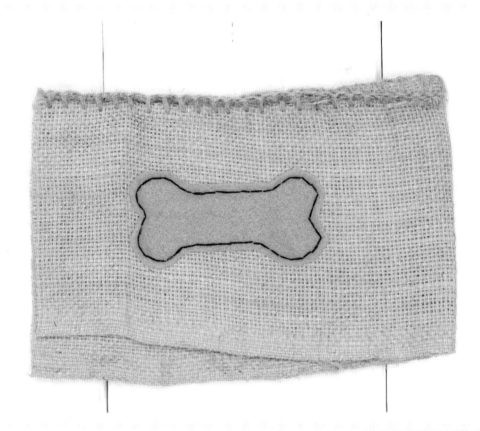

Felt appliqué adds pops and splashes of color to burlap projects. Felt by the yard (meter) or as squares are available in a dazzling array of colors in craft stores. You can draw and then trace your own designs or use cookie cutters as templates. Attach felt to your project using simple stitches—fancy ones are sometimes just too over-the-top for a basic material like burlap—and save your clever needlework stitches to add detail to the felt itself.

You will need

- Burlap or other fabric washed, dried, and ironed as required
- Felt
- Paper and pencil or cookie cutter
- Chalk
- Scissors
- Dressmaking pins
- Embroidery needle and embroidery floss

TIP

Embroidery floss has six strands, and unless you want to achieve a particular look with the thick thread, split the floss in two to give a sewing thread of three strands.

How to do felt appliqué

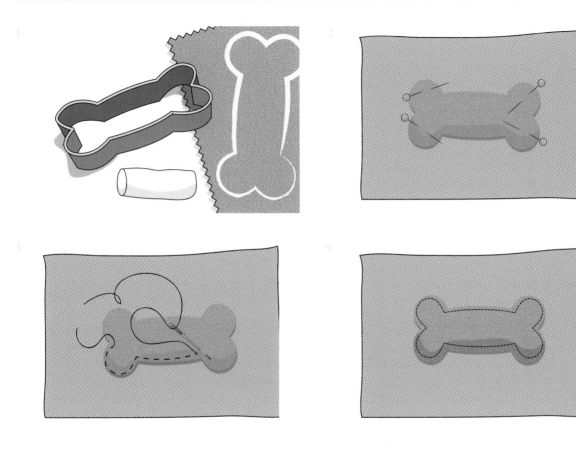

1 Iron the fabric that is to be appliquéd. Trace your design onto the felt with chalk. Cut out the design. If you want to add stitching detail to the felt, do it now.

2 Position the felt onto the fabric and pin in place. When you're happy with the placement, it's time to sew!

3 Thread the needle with three- or six-strand floss. Do not knot the free end of the thread, just leave 3 inches (7.5 cm) trailing on the wrong side of the fabric when you push the needle through to make the first stitch.

4 Stitch just inside the edge of the felt. You can leave even spacing between stitches or create a "solid" line by leaving miniscule space between stitches. When you get to where you started stitching, trim the thread to 3 inches (7.5 cm), and knot it to the other thread.

Further reading

Books

1000 Ideas for Creative Reuse: Remake, Restyle, Recycle, Renew
Garth Johnson (Quarry Books, 2009)

Craft-A-Day: 365 Simple Handmade Projects
Sarah Goldschadt (Quirk Books, 2012)

The Big-ass Book of Crafts
Mark Montano (Gallery Books, 2008)

The Knotting & Braiding Bible: The Complete Guide to Creative Knotting Including Kumihimo, Macramé and Plaiting
Dorothy Wood (David & Charles, 2014)

Upcycling: Create Beautiful Things with the Stuff You Already Have
Danny Seo (Running Press Book Publishers, 2011)

Websites
Look no further for crafty inspiration than the world wide web. Be warned: you could get lost among the millions of craft sites or be totally overwhelmed!

curbly.com: Here you'll find DIYs, design hacks, before and after galleries, and tips. It's a great site for finding out how to make stuff with a little know how, low budget, and minimal time.

designsponge.com: The ultimate website for finding inspiration, seeing amazing transformations, and sourcing tried and tested DIYs.

etsy.com: The marketplace for crafty supplies, how-tos or patterns, upcycling inspiration, and all things handmade. It's not the be all and end all, but it's a pretty big deal.

instagram.com: The newest go-to site for inspiration, including beauty pics, travel shots, and crafts galore. You can also share your own crafty, upcycling adventures with other crafters.

instructables.com: Join the maker movement on this site and discover a wealth of how-tos and meet like-minded people online. Reuse, repurpose, and restyle is the motto.

pinterest.com: This is a site in which you could lose yourself for hours. It can be overwhelming as there are so many ideas and so much inspiration, it may stop you in your tracks. Pin ideas, share your projects, and more but don't let it deter you from creating that special something.

recyclart.org: This site curates reader submissions. It posts before and after photos, a brief rundown of the project, and a link to further details. The main caveat to being featured on this site is that your piece must be created using recycled materials.

snapguide.com: Handy dandy how-to guides for free. Here you'll find awesome step-by-step guides or you can share your own project how-tos. Simple text with photos—easy to follow even for a complete novice.

Suppliers

beadshop.com: If you don't have a local bead shop then try online. You can find beads at craft or dollar stores, but if you want something high-end or very specific, then you may need to shop online.

Dollar stores: Dollar stores are getting bigger and better. You can usually find craft supplies, hardware, jute and hemp, and much more.

Habitat for Humanity ReStores: Find tools, home décor, and hardware on the cheap at any Habitat for Humanity ReStore. It's a great place if you're on a budget, want to reuse instead of buying brand new, or if you want something one-of-a-kind to use in your DIY.

Hardware stores: For some of the DIYs you may have to take the plunge and drop by a hardware store. For pliers, screw-in eyelets, and for framing or hanging needs, plan a visit to Rona, Canadian Tire, or Home Depot outlets.

michaels.com: Shop in person or online for your craft goods. This is a great resource for projects, help, and the right supplies. Plus, there's usually a good coupon deal to help keep your costs down.

Thrift stores: Any local thrift store is the perfect place to find treasures to relove. Peruse yours for frames, vases, or old jewelry to use in your projects.

Glossary

Blanket stitch (or decorative edge stitch): An open stitch that lays on the edge of a piece of raw edged or hemmed fabric. Most frequently seen along the edge of blankets, hence its name.

Burlap: A coarse canvas-like fabric made by weaving jute or hemp. It is most commonly used in the manufacture of shipping sacks.

Buttonhole stitch: A decorative and functional looped stitch that is used along the edge of a material and encloses the raw edge. Though it is visually similar to the blanket stitch, the technique used is slightly different.

Cork: A light brown waterproof material that is obtained from the outer layer of the bark of the cork oak. Cork is available in rolls, sheets, squares, dots, and of course in wine corks!

Cross-stitch: A simple decorative stitch whereby one stitch diagonally criss-crosses another stitch to form an X.

Découpage: This is the art or craft of decorating surfaces or objects with pieces of paper adhered to the surface with white glue.

Fabric glue: A liquid adhesive for attaching fabric to fabric without the need for sewing.

Felt appliqué: An embellishment or ornament made using pieces of felt stitched with embroidery floss to an object or surface. The felt is sometimes decorated with additional stitching.

Hemp: A natural fiber that is extracted from the stem of the cannabis plant. It is used to make rope, fabric, and paper. A very popular cord for macramé work.

Jute: A natural fiber that is most commonly used for making rope, twine, and cloth. Like hemp, it is very popular in macramé crafts.

Macramé: The art or craft of using knotted cord or cords, like jute and hemp, to create a decorative object, jewelry, or a functional item.

Spiral knot (or Chinese ladder knot): A frequently used chain of macramé knots, based on the square knot, that creates a spiral braid.

Square knot: A decorative knot used in many macramé projects, including those in this book.

Stencil: A thin sheet of cardboard or plastic with a design cut out into it. It is placed on a surface and ink or paint is applied into the cut out sections.

White glue (or wood glue or school glue): This glue dries clear and adheres to porous surfaces like wood, paper, cloth, and fibers. Applied diluted, it will waterproof a surface.

Index

Acknowledgments

There are so many people and organizations who helped me through my crafty book adventure to mention and thank. Your support, guidance, knowledge, and well wishes have been immensely appreciated.

Huge gratitude to the publishers and editors of this book. To Isheeta, Tamsin, and Lyn: I am so blessed you found me and asked me to write this book. It was a huge, but exciting undertaking for a crafty, upcycling girl from North Vancouver, Canada. Thank you for being part of this and believing in me.

To my agents, Nigel and Ben at Integral Artists: you are two "kewl" dudes. We're gonna make more awesome crafty stuff happen, my friends.

To the people and organizations who made my DIYs easier by donating good cheer and materials: you ROCK! Thanks also to the Agro Café for the crazy amount of burlap sacks, to the Lions Gate Thrift Shop for so many miscellaneous secondhand treasures, and to the peeps at my local Michael's who helped me with my "out there" questions, dilemmas, and craft meltdowns and disasters.

Loads of thanks and love to the North Vancouver City Library, who got me going on my Crafternoons (upcycling workshops), and especially to all my Crafternoon peeps for crafting with me. To LowerLonsdale.ca and The Makers Nation: thank you for letting me write about craft projects and happenings. Crafting is "da bomb" and crafty peeps definitely make the world a brighter and happier place.

And finally, thanks to my family and friends and to my special someone. To my parents for giving me the best combo of genes a girl could ask for, and yes Dad, I sure did choose well! To my friends: I am filled with gratitude to you all for being so fabulous. And, finally, to my husband, Roly. You really are that something wonderful in my life! You are such a gift, and I spend every day knowing how truly blessed I am to be on this adventure with you. You're my person always and completely.

Happy crafting my crafty peeps!
Denise xo